W9-BUY-541

# THE COLOR PURPLE

## NOTES

*including*
- *Brief Life of the Author*
- *List of Characters*
- *Introduction to the Novel*
- *Critical Commentaries*
- *Character Analyses*
- *Suggested Ideas for Essays*
- *Selected Bibliography*

*by*
*Gloria Rose*
*Georgetown University*

INCORPORATED
LINCOLN, NEBRASKA 68501

**Editor**

*Gary Carey, M.A.*
*University of Colorado*

**Consulting Editor**

*James L. Roberts, Ph.D.*
*Department of English*
*University of Nebraska*

ISBN 0-8220-0308-2
© Copyright 1986
by
**Cliffs Notes, Inc.**
All Rights Reserved
Printed in U.S.A.

**1999 Printing**

Cliffs Notes, Inc.        Lincoln, Nebraska

# CONTENTS

# THE COLOR PURPLE
# Notes

## A BRIEF LIFE OF THE AUTHOR

Alice Walker was born in 1944 in rural Georgia, the youngest child of a sharecropper. When she was eight years old, while playing with two of her older brothers, a copper B.B. pellet hit her in the eye. The accident was traumatic, and Alice changed from being a brassy, self-confident child, interested in doing grown-up things, into a shy, solemn, and solitary girl.

Walker immersed herself in her studies, was consistently excellent in them, and after graduation she won a scholarship to Spelman College, a small prestigious black women's school in Atlanta, Georgia. After two years, Walker left to attend Sarah Lawrence College in Bronxville, New York. There she majored in literature and studied extensively in Latin poetry and history.

Walker graduated from Sarah Lawrence in 1965, and three years later she published a collection of poetry, *Once: Poems.* Her first novel, published in 1970, was *The Third Life of Grange Copeland.* During this time, Walker also held an editorial position at *Ms.* magazine; Gloria Steinem, editor-in-chief at *Ms.*, was extremely encouraging and supportive of Walker's efforts, ideas, and writing. In 1976, *Meridian,* Walker's second novel, the story of a woman fighting for civil rights in the American South, was published.

In 1968, Walker married Mel Leventhal, a human rights lawyer, and they had a daughter, Rebecca, before they were divorced in the early 1970s.

In 1982, Walker received the Pulitzer Prize for Literature for her third novel, *The Color Purple.*

# LIST OF CHARACTERS

## Celie

A young black Georgia girl who faces adulthood believing that she has been raped by her father and that he killed both of their babies. The novel examines her struggle to find love, self-esteem, and continuing courage despite harsh setbacks.

## Nettie

Celie's sister. Celie loves Nettie more than anyone else in the world.

## Fonso

Celie and Nettie's stepfather; shortly after their father is killed, he marries their widowed mother.

## Mr. _____ / Albert

The moody, vicious man whom Fonso chooses as Celie's husband.

## Celie's Mother

She loses her mind after her husband is lynched, mutilated, and burned. After she marries Fonso, she is constantly pregnant and ill.

## Annie Julia

Albert's wife who is killed by her boyfriend while coming home from church.

## Shug (Lilly) Avery

A blues singing, no-nonsense woman who teaches Celie about love and self-esteem.

## Harpo

Albert's misguided, immature son; Sofia's husband.

## Kate and Carrie

Albert's sisters who come to "inspect" Celie and her housekeeping.

## Sofia

The outspoken and independent wife of Harpo.

## Bub

Albert's son; he is in and out of jail frequently.

## Albert's Daddy

A carping, prejudiced man; he dislikes Albert's relationship with Shug Avery.

## Tobias

Albert's toadying brother; he is fascinated by Shug.

## Odessa

Sofia's sister; she, Shug, and Squeak are able to get Sofia out of prison.

## Jack

Odessa's husband.

## Swain

Harpo's musician friend who helps Harpo build the jukejoint.

## Henry ("Buster") Broadax

Sofia's boyfriend; he is tall and stocky, built like a prizefighter.

## Squeak (Mary Agnes)

Harpo's girlfriend; she is a scatterbrained woman who begins to make a name for herself as a blues singer after she leaves Harpo.

## The Mayor

An arrogant, power-wielding white man; he is responsible for putting Sofia in prison.

## Miss Millie

The mayor's wife; a dithery white woman who fancies herself a champion of black people.

## Bubber Hodges

The prison warden; Squeak's uncle who rapes her.

## Miss Beasley

Nettie and Celie's teacher.

## Corrine

Reverend Samuel's wife. She and her husband buy Celie's babies from Fonso.

## Samuel

A missionary who takes Nettie with him and his family to Africa; after his wife, Corrine, dies, he marries Nettie.

## Olivia

Celie's daughter; she is reared in Africa by Samuel and Corrine.

## Adam

Celie's son; he is also reared in Africa by the missionaries. He marries Tashi.

## Joseph

The short, fat spokesman for the Olinka village; he meets Nettie's ship.

## Billy

Miss Millie's little boy; he steps on a rusty nail.

## Eleanor Jane

Miss Millie's daughter; after she is grown, she does baking and odd jobs for Sofia.

## Grady

Shug marries him; he is a "skinny big toof man wearing suspenders," according to Celie.

## May Ellen

The woman Fonso marries after Celie's mother dies.

## Daisy

The woman Fonso marries after May Ellen leaves him.

## Tashi

An Olinka woman whom Adam falls in love with.

## Jimmy Hodges

Bubber's brother; Squeak's father.

## Suzie Q (Jolentha)

Squeak and Harpo's little girl.

## Henrietta

Sofia's youngest child, probably fathered by Henry Broadnax; ironically, Harpo's favorite.

## Jerene and Darlene

Two women who sew for Celie's Folkspants, Unlimited.

## Doris Baines ("Jared Hunt")

An elderly white missionary, whom Nettie and Samuel meet on their sojourn to England. She is accompanied by her "grandchild," Harold, a small black child.

## Germaine

Shug's nineteen-year-old, blues flute playing, last-fling lover.

## Stanley Earl

Eleanor Jane's husband.

## James

Shug's son; a schoolteacher who lives on an Indian reservation; he is married to Cora Mae, and they have two children, Davis and Cantrell.

# INTRODUCTION TO THE NOVEL

*The Color Purple* is not an easy book to read because it is not written in the style of most novels. The author does not tell us everything about the characters and the setting and why the characters behave as they do. This novel consists of a series of letters, none of which are dated, and in order to have a time frame for the novel, we will have to read through it carefully, watching for clues about social attitudes, clothes, and other telling details.

Only after finishing the book do we realize that the letters begin in a time when people ride around in wagons, and when the letters end, people are driving cars. Thus, the time span of the novel is about forty years.

In addition, we soon realize that there are large gaps between letters, sometimes five years, but this information is not revealed by Walker herself. We gather this information from clues within the letters and by comparing letters. Walker does not write as an all-knowing, omniscient narrator, filling in the gaps and giving us background. We must rely on our own close reading and on the details that the women who write the letters – Celie and her sister Nettie – give us.

There is yet another difficulty in reading this novel. We begin with Celie's letters and we encounter a language problem. Celie's letters are not written in standard English. Celie writes her letters in non-standard dialect, what Walker has called black folk language. Thus, at first, Celie's language might seem awkward to some of us, but most readers respond to this novel more immediately if they read the letters aloud, especially Celie's letters, listening to Celie's voice.

Celie is uneducated, and she is writing exactly as she speaks and thinks. There is nothing artificial about her writing "style." In fact, the most distinctive characteristic about Celie's letters is their naturalness. There is a continuous emphasis on the oral sound and sense of what Celie writes, rather than on the "written" style of the letters.

There is also a keen and enduring quality of honesty throughout Celie's letters. She is writing to God, trusting him as she would trust a best friend for guidance and strength to carry on, despite the terrible, painful unhappiness that she feels within her and all those around her.

You should also note that Celie doesn't sign her letters for a long time. This can be explained by realizing that Celie doesn't think of herself as a person of sufficient worth to sign her name. When we meet Celie, she has very little self-confidence. She feels unloved. No one has made her feel valuable. Thus, she turns to God. But even in God's company, Celie feels of little worth.

It will be a long time before Celie gains enough self-esteem to sign her name with pride, but by then, we will have realized that in reading this long series of letters, we have witnessed a wondrous growth of a black woman who was born with all the odds against her. She began life as a virtual slave, the victim of men, of traditional sexual roles, of racism, and of innumerable social injustices. When the novel is finished, we will have seen Celie grow into a whole human being—as well as into a mature, twentieth-century woman.

There are many fine women in this novel, and each of them has a distinctive, fighting sense of courage. They refuse to be beaten into submission. The fiery tempered women, of course, are easily recognized, but it is the quiet, growing strength of Celie that finally impresses us most. For over half the novel, Celie's method of resistance to violence of all kinds is to stoically endure—to pretend that she is wood, a tree bending but not breaking. This psychology works for Celie. For a long time, it is enough. But later, she luckily has friends who convince her that it is not enough to simply endure and "be alive."

One must fight. By nature, Celie is not a fighter. In fact, she refuses to fight until she realizes how thoroughly cruel her husband has been.

For years, Celie "absorbs" Albert's brutal violence, but when she sees proof that he has hidden all of her sister's letters from her, trying to make her think that Nettie was either dead or that she never wrote to her, Celie can take no more. She revolts. She erupts, cursing her husband, and she leaves him to go to Memphis and find happiness with a woman who loves her.

Celie has struggled for many years, keeping alive the memory of Nettie, believing in Nettie, despite the fact that there was no proof that Nettie was alive. It is Celie's courageous spirit that we admire, her fierce, unflagging love for Nettie. And it is Celie's love for Nettie and for Shug that finally allows her to forgive her husband, Albert, for all of his intentional cruelty. Love heals heartaches, and love leads Celie to forgiveness and reconciliation.

When the novel ends, we feel that Celie is "solid" (an adjective that she once used admiringly to describe Sofia). Love has sustained Celie; she has learned to love herself and to share love despite continually cruel pressures. Celie has endured and learned to fight, and she has won her battles. In fact, not only has Celie won, but she has also claimed a sense of joy that she never realized was possible, as well as the knowledge that her strong, constant faith – and her ability to hold on – reunited her with Nettie and with her own children. The family is whole again. Celie has survived – physically and spiritually.

Now, you are ready for the letters. Walker didn't number them, of course. That would have destroyed the verisimilitude of the novel. But for the sake of referring to a particular letter, or for cross-referencing, it is convenient to number the letters in the book itself, numbering each *complete* letter. **Do not number letters within letters.** To double-check your numbering, note that Celie writes Letters 1–51. Nettie's letters begin with Number 52. The letters should end with Number 90.

Above all, don't neglect the opportunity to read aloud as many of Celie's letters as possible. The humor, the love, the pain, and, finally, the faith that sustains Celie are found in her simple, unaffected phrases. By reading Celie's letters aloud, you re-create her voice, and a connection is established between you and this woman who offers you a chance to understand suffering and the need for compassion.

# CRITICAL COMMENTARIES

## Letter 1

Celie, a nearly illiterate black Georgia girl, writes a short note to God, confiding to him that she's only fourteen, but already she is burdened with cooking, cleaning, and caring for a multitude of brothers and sisters because of her mother's failing health. In addition, her father has raped her.

We are stunned. Seldom has a novel begun so melodramatically — and yet so briefly and in such a matter-of-fact style. We are caught off-guard. Clearly, this letter to God is not a prayer, as one might expect a letter to God to be. But, on the other hand, despite the sexual violence described in the letter, there is nothing excessively melodramatic about the letter in terms of its style. In fact, what we notice, first of all, and perhaps most important, is the fact that Celie is writing to God in much the way that she would write to, or speak to, a good, close, loving friend. This letter, written in what Walker has called black folk language, contains a strong and sustained sense of naturalness throughout.

Talking to her friend God, Celie uses the words "titties," "pussy," and "his thing" without any sense of embarrassment. These words are the only words that Celie knows for these terms. Celie is an innocent young girl who has been sexually abused by her father, and now she is confused as to why it happened to her. So she asks all-knowing God: *why?* And in telling God what has happened, there is nothing shocking about her language because it is the natural language of this black girl. What is shocking is the fact that her father has raped her and has threatened more violence if she tells anyone about it. The violence itself is shocking — not Celie's language.

The reason why Celie writes to God is that she would like to tell her mother what happened, but Celie's father has warned her not to — to tell "nobody but God," *especially not* Celie's mother because, according to him, "It'd kill your mammy."

Again, we are caught off-guard. We know that this novel is written by a contemporary black woman, and therefore, the word "mammy" is jarring. Usually we encounter "mammy" only in so-called soft-core racist songs and literature. For example, we think of the song "Mammy's Li'l Baby Loves Shortnin' Bread," and we also think of all of the turbaned, sassy, protective "mammies" who (according to the movies) ruled Southern plantation kitchens, as well as most of the rest of the plantation house affairs, and, of course, we recall Al Jolson's "black face," sung-on-bended-knee version of "Mammy," and scores of other instances where the word "mammy" is used in a condescending, put-down, racist context. "Mammy" does not have a positive connotation to today's progressive black and white ears.

Yet here, Celie's father uses the term, and obviously, it is as natural to him as his untamed need for sex is. So, not only are prudish readers caught off-guard by Walker's language concerning Celie's rape, but so are black and white liberals when Walker, very naturally, within the context of this novel, introduces a word that has evolved into a racist term. Walker begins this novel, as one critic has noted, with exactly the same ingredients that a Greek playwright would have used for the climax of his tragedy.

We realize, then, that Celie is too scared to tell her mother, or her mammy, what her father has done, so she has told no one. She wants to be a "good girl," and she knows that if she lets her father rape her, he will leave her sick mother alone. Celie abhors her father's rough, sexual brutality, but by submitting to it, she spares her mother. Note that Celie tells God, "She happy"—that is, to Celie's mother, sickness seems far preferable to Fonso's (Celie's father's) brutality.

In addition, Celie is telling God that sexual violence should not be her reward for having been (and she emphasizes that she has been) a "good girl." She asks God for a "sign" to let her know "what is happening." She feels that she's being punished, that somehow she's to blame, and she doesn't understand why. She hopes that a sign from God will explain why she is suffering—from rape, incest, and so much sudden responsibility. Celie, of course, doesn't know these words—rape, incest, and responsibility—yet. She knows only that she is struggling to endure—to hold on—during this crisis. She is troubled, and in terrible pain, and is deeply confused. And in addition, she feels utterly alone. Therefore, she writes to someone whom she trusts—God, asking for understanding and explanation.

## Letter 2

In Celie's first letter to God, she referred to herself as a girl, in the sense that she was chronologically a girl and, moreover, she emphasized that she was a "good girl." Other children who are Celie's age may still be literally and chronologically "girls," but we realize here that Celie is a woman. At fifteen, she is pregnant and she is carrying er father's child. Moreover, Celie's current pregnancy is not even Celie's first pregnancy.

Celie has already had another baby – a year ago, when she was fourteen. What happened to it? Celie's mother asks this question on her deathbed, and Celie answers that "God took it." She loves her mother so much that she wants her to think that the baby was still-born.

This is not what Celie believes in her heart, however. She believes that her father, and the baby's father, Fonso, killed the baby, but because Celie's mother dies such a painful, loud death, with Fonso moaning and sitting beside the bed, and with Celie nursing and caring for the other children, what else can Celie do but lie? She doesn't want to hurt her mother, and, in addition, we see that Celie fears that Fonso will kill this second baby, just as he did the first one. She doesn't want to burden her mother, as she is dying, with this terrible knowledge.

Celie's compassion for her mother is clearly not that of a "girl"; she has the understanding and compassion of a woman. Celie's child-bearing and her witnessing the agonizing death of her mother have forced her to become a woman long before her time.

Celie's mother dies, screaming at Celie and cursing her, and yet Celie never tells her that Fonso is the father of both babies.

Unfortunately, with her mother gone, Celie has no protection from her father's sexual attacks. And since we, the readers, realize this, Fonso's pleas to his wife of "don't leave me, don't go" seem fraudulent. How could a man "cherish" his wife and sexually abuse their daughter – and then slay his own child? Perhaps he wants to con-ceal his incestuous relationship with his daughter. Perhaps he wants to decrease the number of mouths he has to feed. At present, his motivations are unclear. But at this point, we are not deeply concerned with Fonso's motivations. We are far more concerned with Celie's plight: living with a father who rapes her, expecting another baby, and living with the almost certainty that her father killed their first child.

These first two letters to God are some of the most powerful letters in American literature, and certainly no other major American novel has begun with such unexpected narrative dynamite.

## Letter 3

In this letter, Walker focuses on two key ideas: first, Celie tells

God that she thinks that Fonso took his and Celie's second child, a boy, and sold it to a childless couple. Note here that Celie is relieved that her baby has been sold. Again we are stunned; theoretically, selling black children went out with the abolition of slavery. But we hear this young woman confess to happiness that this extraordinary, inhuman act of "salvation" has, in fact, happened to her baby. This is Walker's way of emphasizing the fact that life with Fonso is a deadly nightmare. Celie is grateful that her baby is far away from Fonso's vicious temper. We realize also that Fonso still has not told Celie precisely what he did with their first baby. At this point in the novel, Fonso seems little more than a one-dimensional, evil and wicked villain.

Celie's happiness because of her new baby's safety is short-lived because she herself is left with unneeded milk in her breasts, and she has no decent clothes to wear. As a result, Fonso becomes hateful and acts "like he can't stand me no more." Accordingly, Fonso's sexual lust turns from Celie to her younger sister Nettie.

Celie's adult-like concern for her younger sister Nettie is the second focus in this letter to God. Celie doesn't want Nettie to be sexually brutalized as she herself has been. She hopes that her father will find a new wife soon because she senses that with a new "mother" around, they will all be happier. Interestingly, Celie's having to act like a mother to Nettie at this time is ironic because of the fact that both girls are so close in age – and yet Celie has already had two children, but both babies have been taken from her; she has never had a chance to be a "real," loving, nurturing mother – except to Nettie.

We see from this letter that Celie still has an incredibly strong faith in God, and selfless as ever, Celie vows to use his help to protect not herself, but to protect Nettie. Celie's selflessness and her lack of lasting bitterness are proof that she is, and will remain, a strong Christian woman. In summary, note again that Celie is not sad about the fate of her second child; as Walker emphasizes, Celie feels glad that her baby is far away from the evil Fonso. Now Celie has only Nettie to worry about. Not herself, but Nettie. And Celie promises Nettie in this letter to God that she will "take care of you . . . with God help."

## Letter 4

Here, we discover that God has seemingly fulfilled Celie's hopes.

Celie tells him that her father has married a woman about sixteen years old who comes from a neighboring town. They have sex frequently, and Celie's new stepmother has taken over the responsibility for all of Fonso's children. We can conclude from this statement that, at last, Nettie is safe from Fonso's brutal sexuality.

But Nettie, who is about fifteen, while not being victimized by her father, is being courted by an older widower, a man with three children. Moreover, Celie says that the man resembles Fonso, and she tells God that his first wife was murdered on her way home from church—"kilt by her boyfriend." Again, we unexpectedly encounter extraordinary violence. Yet Celie seems to accept this violence as a natural, ever-present, if unpleasant, part of life. We read these short letters almost in disbelief because of the matter-of-fact way that Celie describes what is jarringly tragic—to us.

Of course, Celie doesn't encourage the relationship between Nettie and the widower; she urges Nettie to use her energies on studying. She doesn't want Nettie to end up dead like their mother, from too much hard work and too many pregnancies.

The bond between Celie and Nettie is a bond of unusually deep love. Yet, except for the love that Celie and Nettie share, and the love that God offers to the women here, there is a painful lack of love; in its place, there is a sense of paralyzed doom in this household. The fates of the new stepmother, Nettie, and Celie all seem inescapable. They all have to toil endlessly, and their only relief lies in going to church and believing in an afterlife, and therefore, the key sentence in this particular letter is "All needing something."

In an extension of its literal meaning, we realize that all three of the women, and all of the other children as well, *need*. They need material things. But especially the women need more than material things. They need respect and understanding and love. There are no black men to give these women the respect and the understanding and, most of all, the love that they need. Only God offers them love, and in Celie and Nettie's case, they offer love to one another.

Finally, note that Celie deliberately chooses not to tell God the name of her new stepmother, nor does she tell him the name of Nettie's suitor. This namelessness is indicative of the universality of these people, as well as a lack of any real, personal, mature identity. Celie doubtlessly knows what her new stepmother and Nettie's suitor represent: pain and suffering in their own lives, as well as pain and suffering in the lives they interact with.

## Letter 5

In this letter to God, Celie confides that life is still unjust; Fonso has beat her for flirting in church. Flirting with men, Celie tells God, is something completely foreign to her nature. She is frightened of men – and for good cause. The men in her life have been brutal and callous. Celie doesn't even "look" at men. Instead, she looks at women. She trusts women; she forgives even her mother for the mad, raving verbal attacks described in Letter 2.

We should realize at this point that a pattern of physical abuse is being established and repeated. As far as Celie knows, her mother never enjoyed her ever-pregnant life. This is why Celie urges Nettie to try for a little happiness with her suitor, Mr. _____. To Celie, even "one good year" seems like a very long time to be happy. "One good year" means one year in which Nettie won't be beaten or be pregnant. And Celie herself supposes that she is pregnant again because she hasn't been having regular menstrual periods. Celie has had two children, but she doesn't fully understand the process of conception. No one has explained to her the workings of a woman's body – just as no one has offered her love and understanding.

## Letter 6

In this letter, we realize that Celie may be unschooled, but that she has a deep intuitive sense; we will see evidence of this throughout the book. For example, Celie isn't convinced that Fonso's objections to Nettie's marrying Mr. _____ have anything to do with the truth of the matter. Celie's intuitive bent zeroes in on the name of Shug Avery, when Fonso mentions Shug as a possible reason why he won't let Nettie marry Mr. _____.

Thus, we are introduced to one of the major characters in the novel – perhaps the one person who will emerge as the greatest influence on Celie's learning to love herself – and other people. Shug Avery is Mr. _____'s mistress. That's all we know at present, and even that fact is only hinted at. But note that although the "introduction" of this character is just suggested for the present, Walker is creating dramatic tension and suspense even before a photograph of Shug is shown to Celie.

In a way, Shug's being introduced later by a photograph is proof that she belongs to an "outside world." Celie's world contains no beauty, and Celie is immediately conscious of the fact that Shug is "the most beautiful woman I ever saw." She even says that Shug is prettier than "my mama." Celie's comparison of Shug to her mother is no accident. This is Walker's way of foreshadowing; she is suggesting that Shug may soon become a mother figure and a role model, as well as a source of love – to replace, and finally even to surpass, Celie's love for her mother.

In her previous letter to God, Celie said, "I look at women" (and not at men). Here, her close scrutiny and admiration of Shug are clear evidence of the truth of Celie's statement. Because there is a beautiful woman named Shug Avery, Celie no longer feels that she and her world are just plain and simple. She can now dream of something rich and beautiful. Dreams of Shug Avery will provide beauty in Celie's life. Shug will represent fanciness in style, freedom in spirit, and many extraordinary fantasies in Celie's dreary, painful life.

## Letter 7

This letter emphasizes the fact that Celie is powerless to refuse to marry any man whom Fonso chooses as her husband. And Fonso is ready to get rid of her. Celie offers herself to Fonso, instead of Nettie, so that he can have sex while his new wife is sick. Fonso, of course, uses Celie and then he arrogantly says in Celie's presence that she is a "bad influence on my other girls." He says that Celie "ain't fresh" (isn't a virgin) and that she is "spoiled. Twice" (that is, Celie has had two children). Motherhood is a dirty word in Fonso's mouth; this is further proof that Fonso has no feeling for Celie's (and other women's) sensitivity.

To Fonso, Nettie has replaced Celie in the home. To Fonso, Celie is nothing more than an aging beast of burden that must be disposed of because "the master" is now tired of it. Fonso's comments underscore this; he "praises" Celie to Mr. _____, but note how he does it. Celie, he says, "work like a man." He also tells Mr. _____ that Celie can't bear children anymore and, therefore, Mr. _____ can use Celie sexually any way he wants to and Celie won't "make you feed it or clothe it." What he is saying is this: Mr. _____ can rape Celie any time and any way he pleases and he doesn't have to worry about Celie getting pregnant. Fonso even offers to include a cow in the bargain if Mr. _____ will marry Celie. Later, when Mr. _____ decides to come for Celie, it seems as though it was the cow that made the difference.

Because Fonso has nothing positive to say about Celie, she very naturally turns her thoughts to a woman who is a beautiful woman. Celie studies the picture of Shug Avery. The image and personality of Shug have extended by now beyond the photograph and have so permeated Celie's imagination that she can even hear Shug's voice. Shug "seems" to say to Celie, "Yeah, it bees that way sometime," uttering a folk axiom which expresses a universal truth that "whatever is, is." But there is no cynicism or bitterness in the statement; there is simply Celie's stoic country knowledge that while Shug lives in a magical world, Celie herself must accept her poor, meager condition. Ironically, however, it will be Shug who will prove to Celie that life need not always be hopeless.

## Letter 8

The significance of this letter lies in its rendering of the especially close relationship that exists between Nettie and Celie. Nettie's trying to persuade their father into letting Celie attend school is strong evidence of her deep, maternal compassion for her sister and her concern for her sister's future.

Celie is about twenty years old when Mr. _____ returns to take "another look" at her; he appraises her from horseback, much as he would reckon the worth of a farm animal, and then he decides to take her—after Fonso reassures him that a cow is included in the bargain.

Despite the depressing thoughts about what Celie's future might hold, there is one light note: Nettie and Celie have a delightful exchange about the world not being round. To Celie, the world seems literally flat—and metaphorically flat, made up of unending misery and monotony. But Celie doesn't tell Nettie this; it is important to Celie that Nettie continue to think that she isn't dumb.

## Letter 9

Here, we realize that Celie doesn't write to God about packing her things, or about her wedding ceremony, or even about moving into a new home. Her opening lines concern violence: "I spend my wedding day running from the oldest boy." On Celie's wedding day, this twelve-year-old hellion, who will be her stepson, bashes her in the head with a rock. Celie bandages her head and begins to function automatically, revealing that she accepts the fact that this chaos and violence will probably be a pattern throughout the rest of her life. It will be a pattern that she will simply have to cope with.

There is nothing "special" about Celie's wedding day until nighttime, when she is dutifully lying beneath Mr. _____. Then, she unselfishly and lovingly thinks of Nettie's welfare. Now that Nettie and Celie are separated, they can no longer try to protect one another. Celie's thoughts are of Nettie, even in this wretched, perhaps hopeless situation. Celie does not dwell on self-pity.

Then Celie thinks of Shug, and Shug seems closer than ever to Celie because Celie realizes that she and Shug share the same man. Celie, "that one" whom Fonso said was ugly, is sharing her husband with the exotic and wondrous Shug Avery. Logically, Celie reasons that this act of sex with Mr. _____ must please Shug, and because Celie deeply desires to be like Shug, she begins to embrace Mr. _____, but all of her thoughts continue to dwell on the beautiful Shug Avery.

## Letter 10

Celie's trip into town with Mr. _____ is exciting and stimulating for her because, as a country woman, she has a chance to observe these seemingly sophisticated townspeople: "I never seen so many even at church. Some be dress too."

The townspeople, however, are not sophisticated. They drive into town in wagons, and we don't see them buying readymade clothes; they buy material and thread. And their attitudes are certainly not educated ones. Likewise, the whites in town are not sophisticated either. Specifically, the clerk's demeaning treatment of Olivia's mother and Celie reflects his contradictory and self-defeating behavior: he needs their business, but he clearly hates blacks, for his words to them are rude and pushy: "You want that cloth or not? We got other customers sides you."

Although little Olivia's mother is a woman, the clerk calls her a "girl," and he calls Celie a "gal." His forcing the woman to purchase unneeded thread is linked to his treating her like a child. To him, the woman has no judgment. "You can't sew thout thread."

One of the most telling sentences in this letter is Celie's saying, "I don't have nothing to offer and I feels poor." Ironically, Celie offers the woman a great deal. She offers her friendship and a kind word, and she generously offers them to this woman who is holding Olivia, the baby whom Celie *feels* is her own baby. In addition, Celie offers the woman a seat in Mr. _____'s wagon when the woman can't see the Reverend's wagon. In turn, Olivia's mother offers Celie a joke about Celie's "*horse*pitality." Celie's joy soars. She laughs until her face feels ready to split, "laughing like a fool," Mr. _____ calls it. She laughs because she feels almost certain that she has found her baby.

Olivia's mother also laughs, and this is a relief for us after we have seen her overly submissive behavior earlier. But the woman acts so passively in this scene because she knows that she has no choice. In a confrontation with a white man, the black man, or woman, must act passively. Their survival depends upon not angering whites. In fact, the woman's over-politeness is proof of this point, as is the fact that she allows the clerk to humiliate her and take her money.

In contrast to the clerk, Celie is careful to keep the woman's pride intact. She compliments her on the fabric. But Celie is too curious about the baby to be quiet for too long. She asks about the baby's father and learns that he is a Reverend. Celie doesn't tell God his name; she leaves him nameless. Walker first employed this technique in Letter 4 to express a lack of personal identity. Celie again repeats the notion that a man's name is not worth knowing — because "mens look pretty much alike to me." There is a certain element of irony in this scene, inherent in the fact that an allegedly incestuously begotten child is now the daughter of a minister.

Celie's second question to the woman reveals her intuitive nature even more clearly. She asks her, "How long you had your little girl?" and here, note the verb "had." This is not the usual way to ask someone how old a child is. The verb "had" carries the idea that the baby was gotten from somewhere besides the womb of the woman who holds her.

In addition, there is the matter of the baby's name being Olivia or Pauline. The name "Olivia" is a secret, private name which both women have for the baby. Celie, of course, embroidered Olivia's name in her underwear, which went with her when Fonso sold her. Olivia's mother has no real answer as to why she calls the baby Olivia; rather embarrassed, she says that the baby simply "look like a Olivia."

We have some evidence, then, that this baby may be Celie's baby, discovered by chance; but for the present, Celie cannot be absolutely sure. Yet, she *feels* that the baby is hers. She tells God, "My heart say she mine." This notion of Celie's listening more and more to her heart, and trusting her feelings, will take on increasing importance throughout the rest of the novel.

## Letter 11

Nettie's running away from home to Mr. _____'s house reunites the sisters and helps bond them even more firmly together with sustaining love. Nettie is able to help her overworked sister with the household chores and, more important, with her schooling. Nettie deeply wants to teach, and Celie is deeply appreciative of Nettie's patience and belief in her: "No matter what happen, Nettie steady try to teach me what go on in the world." At the same time, however, the constant labor of being a mother to Mr. _____'s four children (and not three as he said earlier) has taken a bite out of Celie's will. Most days, she tells God, she's too tired even to think.

In keeping with the basic selflessness in their relationship, the sisters continue to worry about each other's welfare. Nettie regrets having to leave Celie, saying that it's like seeing her buried. Even Nettie's idealism is tested severely in this scene. Celie, however, draws on her faith to provide her daily resurrection. She states firmly that as long as she can "spell G-o-d I got somebody along." The verb "spell" in this sentence is a clue to us that Celie will continue to write her letters to God and not decide to "think them" in a different kind of narrative form. Accordingly, she begins the following letter, Letter 12, not with her customary Dear God, but with G-o-d spelled out.

Nettie, then, is largely responsible for Celie's being able to write these letters to God. Learning is synonymous with strength to Nettie, and she continually urges Celie to learn to be strong, to fight – and not to succumb to the "taken-for-granted" burdens of the black woman's role. Nettie promises to write, but Celie ends this letter by saying that Nettie never wrote.

This matter will be addressed in Letter 49. Celie is not aware of the irony in this final, short sentence. Celie won't read any of the letters that Nettie wrote to her for a very long time, but when she does, they will structure the second half of this novel.

## Letter 12

After the pain of most of the preceding letters, this letter seems almost like comic relief. Mr. _____'s two sisters come to inspect the new bride, and they gossip like a pair of nosey neighbors about what a tacky person their brother's first wife was (the one who was killed by her boyfriend coming home from church). They are inflexibly rigid about a "woman's role." To them, women get married and are supposed to keep a "decent house" and a "clean family." They are a pair of very critical women, and because Celie is sensitive enough to read between the lines of their comments, she surely must feel proud and relieved by their comments; she has favorably impressed the two sisters. She has their approval—as a good housekeeper, as a person who is good with children, and as a good cook. And note how Walker slips a memory of Nettie into Celie's thoughts. Kate says that her brother couldn't have done better in getting himself a wife "if he'd tried." Celie calmly remarks to God, "I think about how he tried." That is, Mr. _____ wanted Nettie first and foremost; he took Celie only after considering that he'd get a cow in the bargain.

The two sisters' presence, however, is more than comic relief in this scene. These sisters are going to offer more information about this magical creature called Shug Avery. They don't think much of Shug because, according to them, Shug can't sing, she's a homebreaker, and, according to Kate, Shug is "black as my shoe."

The adjective "black" means that not only is Shug a member of the black race, but that she has a very dark black complexion. Because of miscegenation, skin tone among black Americans varies from milky to ebony. Some black people have attached status to being lighter and have avoided darker members of the race. The roots for this colorist distinction come from slavery. Lighter persons who were frequently the offspring of white masters and black women slaves were given the easier work—usually the housework. The rest of the slaves, the darker ones, were given the fieldwork to do.

Carrie's sharp-tongued observation about Shug—"She too black"—means that Shug's skin tone is probably close to ebony. However, all this prejudice refuses to take root in Celie's consciousness; she is more intrigued than ever by the illusive Shug Avery. In fact, now that Shug is the personification of adventure and magic and beauty, Celie associates a shopping trip with the glamorous Shug. It also seems that Celie knows that purple is associated with royalty; that's why she says "purple" aloud when she and Kate are discussing the color of Celie's new dress. Celie is thinking of Shug and simply utters the color that is synonymous with Shug: purple. But just as there is no Shug Avery in Celie's life – not yet – there is no color purple in the dress store. Not yet. For the present, Celie has to make do with blue. But Kate utters one of the central ideas in this novel that becomes a part of Celie's soul. She tells Celie that she deserves "more than this." And Celie timidly agrees with Kate. "Maybe so. I think."

Later, Kate is unsuccessful when she tries to make Harpo share the house chores with Celie, but she doesn't leave before she tells Celie the same thing which Nettie told her: Celie must "fight them." And then she utters words which are more powerful than perhaps even she herself realizes. She tells Celie to "fight them for yourself." Celie, of course, isn't ready to fight yet. For the present, simply *not giving up* is enough for her. At least, she is alive. Nettie, she fears, is dead. But Kate's words have been spoken, and Celie will hear other women tell her the same thing throughout the novel – to "fight them for yourself" – because Celie is worth it. Slowly, Celie will begin to realize the truth of this statement.

## Letter 13

About five years have passed. Harpo was twelve when he gashed Celie's head on her wedding day; now he is seventeen. Celie is about twenty-five, and Mr. _____ has just beaten her again. Mr. _____'s answer about why he beats Celie is tyrannical; in essence, he states that Celie is stubborn and she is a woman, and all women are good for is for beating, and wives are especially good for beating.

Harpo is confused, and Celie is reminded of her father's own irrational, unexplainable cruelty. She, however, has no alternative, seemingly, than accepting her "role" as a black woman: she is merely a black man's "property"; accordingly, she is an available target for all the abuse that her husband has boiling inside himself. Mr. _____ suffered frustration and unhappiness from his late wife, Annie Julia, and now he suffers frustration because of Shug Avery, his current mistress. And, of course, he suffers frustration because he is a black man, a man of little value in the white man's world.

Celie feels humiliated because she is treated worse than even his children. But Mr. _____ unknowingly articulates a quality of Celie's that will grow into full-fledged revolt one day: her stubbornness. He says, self-righteously, that Celie is "stubborn." He is not punishing Celie for any specific act she has done, but because she stands up to him and to life and reminds him of times when he himself was not stubborn and resilient to life's injustices. Celie only knows that, as she said at the end of Letter 12, "I don't fight. . . . but I'm alive," and then she reveals to God how she manipulates her emotions while being abused by her husband. She imagines that she is as strong and as unmoving as a tree. "I make myself wood. . . . Celie, you a tree."

Celie, then, is still uncertain about why she is physically abused, and there is another person who is also "uncertain" in this chapter: Harpo. He thinks that he's ready to get married, but he is as ignorant about love and sexuality and courtship as Celie was when she first began writing her letters to God. Harpo is seventeen, but he seems much younger because he is so certain that he loves a girl whom he has never even spoken to; indeed, it is his very certainty that makes him seem all the more immature. The two young people, as we pointed out, have never even spoken; they have merely exchanged a wink and returned a scared, shy look. Yet, to Harpo, this is "love," and he is sure that he's ready to be a husband. But with Harpo's having a fierce father for a role model as a husband, we can be fairly certain that Harpo will probably become another womanizer and a wife beater. Another cycle of brutality, it seems, is innocently and ignorantly being set in motion.

## Letter 14

This letter is filled with Celie's ecstatic anticipation of Shug Avery's coming to town—even though Celie herself won't be going to hear Shug's performance. Nevertheless, Celie aches just to see, "just to lay eyes on" this beautiful creature from seemingly another world (another star in the universe). Symbolically, note that Shug will be singing at the Lucky Star club; Shug will eventually be Celie's "lucky star."

It is completely natural that Mr. _____ would expect Celie to help him look his very best for "the other woman," his mistress, Shug. To him, Celie is more a slave than a wife. But Celie doesn't mind this time because she wants Mr. _____ to see Shug so that she can learn

more about her. She has been living vicariously through Mr. _____
when he is with Shug.

In Letter 6, Celie saw Shug in a single snapshot. Now, Celie sees
that Mr. _____ has sixty pink announcements, with pictures of
Shug, billed as the Queen Honeybee; he has nailed many of the pink
posters to the trees like a myriad of exotic pink butterflies. Magic
reigns, and the queen of this magic is the Queen Honeybee – Shug
Avery. Her name is the first syllable of the word "sugar," and the word
"honeybee" carries the idea of hot and stinging sweetness. Shug is a
blues singer, and no doubt she was referred to as a "sugar babe," a
common and affectionate term for a black woman blues singer.

## Letter 15

Celie's earthy wisdom, in contrast to her child-like innocence,
underscores every line of this short note to God. That is, Celie knows
that her husband has a mistress, but she accepts the situation matter-
of-factly; at the same time, she never once questions herself (as most
women would) about why she herself isn't considered as valuable to
her husband as his mistress is. Celie has a tragically small amount
of self-worth. To Celie, all worth lies in Shug Avery. Celie knows so
little about the true, objective worth of herself that she accepts the
fact that her husband has so much sex with Shug that he's totally
exhausted and almost sick when he returns home. Celie is grateful
for crumbs; so long as she can share her husband with the fantastic
Shug Avery, she can cope with life.

In the meantime, while her husband has been with Shug, Celie
has worked like a mule in the fields, and she's done so for one reason
only: she knows that she's expected to – "it bees that way." Celie accepts
her narrowly defined, sexist, racist, black woman's role almost will-
ingly, so long as she can dream of the glamorous Shug Avery and
Shug's clothes, hair, and makeup. Celie even knows that Shug and
Mr. _____ have children, but she is not jealous – "it bees that way."
Having access to Shug through Mr. _____ is enough. Celie and
Shug have the relationship of picture and viewer, book and reader,
and performer and audience. In fact, to Celie, Shug seems like a
character in a familiar fairy tale: "Is she still the same old Shug, like
in my picture?" Without having ever met Shug Avery, the idea of Shug
is electrically real ("like snakes") to Celie.

## Letters 16 & 17

The focus in these letters is mostly on Harpo. Celie talks about all the hard field work which she and Harpo have done since Mr. _____ returned in a stupor from his rendezvous with Shug. Celie is sensitive to the fact that Harpo is nearly as big and strong as his daddy, yet, contradictorily, "weak in will." Her voice is tender as she describes Harpo's sad and thoughtful eyes.

Part of Harpo's sadness, of course, comes from his being in love, but a good part of it comes as a result of his being a black man, toiling until exhausted in the fields. Also, in Letter 17, we learn that Mr. _____ has told Harpo that the nightmarish scandal of his mother's murder hangs over Harpo, and that it makes him "unfit" as a suitor for his girlfriend.

In Harpo's nightmare of his mother, Annie Julia is torn between Harpo and her lover, symbols of responsibility versus desire. Fatally, she chooses to be a responsible mother.

Harpo's response is to cry out against the injustice of his mother's death. His mother was *not* to blame, and yet everyone in the community did blame her – because she let her desires seek gratification. And at this point, Harpo's cry of injustice reverberates in echoes, recalling all of the injustices that have been mentioned in all of Celie's letters to God – particularly all of the multiple injustices that have stunted Celie's (Harpo's stepmother's) rightful sense of herself.

Celie's selflessness here, thinking only of Harpo, is almost saint-like. She realizes now that she can never replace Annie Julia, Harpo's mother, just as she herself knew so well, long ago, that Fonso's new wife could never replace Celie's own mother.

As a stepmother herself now, Celie knows for a certainty that she doesn't love Mr. _____'s children, and yet that realization does not deter her from acting lovingly toward them. This contradiction in not loving but acting lovingly, as well as the many contradictions of justice and injustice that Celie witnesses every day, coalesce finally in Celie's thoughts about the contradictory nature of Harpo's unwed, pregnant girlfriend, Sofia. Sofia, Celie says, is gentle, yet strong – pregnant and unwed, yet not troubled about the fact. To Celie, Sofia's headstrong, contradictory independence is simply one more fact to be reckoned with. But to Harpo and Mr. _____, Sofia's headstrong independence is an alien and frightening omen.

## Letters 18–21

Celie never learns, or at least she doesn't tell God, what finally persuades Sofia to marry Harpo and make a home for him and their baby boy. But once they are settled, Celie studies this strange black woman who is unlike any woman whom Celie has ever known. Celie's word for Sofia is "solid." It is a quality that Celie is clearly unfamiliar with, because, at one point, childlike Celie tells Harpo to beat Sofia. Seemingly, Celie wants to see if Sofia will break.

Sofia, of course, doesn't break – but Celie has never been broken either – except in Celie's case, everyone assumes that her will has already been broken, if indeed it ever existed. Celie may act submissive, however, but she has always reacted to beatings, without knowing it, in much the same way that Sofia does. Objectively, one can see that Sofia is "solid." No one suspects, however, that when Celie is beaten, she too is "solid"; she imagines that she is wood and absorbs the violence inflicted on her – but she doesn't break or become bitter. In her own words, she says stoically, "I don't fight . . . but I'm alive."

When Harpo attempts to break Sofia's will, he is clearly the bruised loser, and note here how humorously, and yet how all too accurately, he explains that he had a run-in with a mule. Consider Sofia and the theoretical mule. Sofia and a mule are not too different. Both must do fieldwork and both are stubborn. Also, a mule is as much a female as it is a male. And Sofia is as much a woman as she is a man. She is both a mother and a fighter.

Year after year, Harpo continues to try and tame Sofia, and yearly, he loses – bruised but stubbornly determined to make his woman a slave to him. Finally, Celie witnesses Harpo's bruises one time too many, and deep guilt festers within her Christian soul; she knows that it was she, along with Mr. _____, who urged Harpo to beat Sofia in the first place.

Letter 21, then, is a key letter; it contains one of the most significant scenes in the novel: Sofia confronts Celie. Sofia has learned that Celie told Harpo to beat her, and she reveals how terribly betrayed she feels. It is one thing to have a man try to beat you; it is quite another thing to have a woman betray another woman. Sofia trusted Celie because Celie seemed like a kind woman. Sofia believed that there was a special bond between them, as women, and now she has learned that a woman urged a man to do her harm. A woman should know better; as Sofia says, "A girl child ain't safe in a family of men."

This raw exchange between the two women is significant because of their well-defined, vividly contrasting characters. Sofia is a fighter — loudly independent and sharply decisive. Celie is a timid shadow — quietly anguished as she admits to having been a fool. Sofia cannot understand Celie's motivation; both women were reared in similar domestic situations, but Sofia has always been filled with angry aggressiveness, diametrically unlike the passive, mother-like, spiritual Celie. Sofia's advice to Celie is loud and clear: "You ought to bash Mr. _____ head open. Think about heaven later."

Laughing together, the two women are reconciled finally because there has been an honest exchange of viewpoints between them, and their reconciliation is symbolized by the quilt that they decide to make together. A quilt, after all, is a collection of many colors and fabrics sewn by a single thread, and the new union between Celie and Sofia will be sewn with a new, strong thread of love and trust.

## Letters 22–27

Finally, after years of hearing about, thinking about, and dreaming about the fantastic Shug Avery, Celie is at last going to meet Shug. Walker has classically constructed an "entrance scene" for Shug — that is, novelists and playwrights often like to create intense interest and curiosity about a major character before the reader (or viewer) "sees" that character. We, the readers or the audience, hear about this character from several viewpoints; we see a painting or a picture of the character, and thus we are psychologically "baited," anxiously awaiting this person who obviously plays a major role in other people's lives but who has not, as yet, been on stage.

In this case, we are fascinated by this Queen Honeybee, this high-stepping, blues moaning, good looking, sensuous jazz singer who is, to Mr. _____ and to Celie, everything that Celie is not. We have grown fond of Celie and have identified with her mistreatment and her loneliness; now we are at last going to meet a person who has hypnotically fascinated both Celie and Mr. _____. How, we wonder, can this magnetic woman hold such emotional power over two people so diametrically dissimilar as Celie and Mr. _____?

First off, in analyzing Shug Avery, we should note that Shug may be the Queen Honeybee in the jazz club where she sings, but obviously she reigns only while she sings. In this scene, she is ill, but no one offers to take care of her. On her own turf, she may be a queen of sorts, but her turf is a land of booze-and-blues, sort of an unreal after-hours Never-Never-Land, where the queen isn't supposed to get sick like real folks do. Shug's audience only loves her when she sings, and her lovers only enjoy her while they are in bed with her. In the bright light of day, the Queen Honeybee's outspoken individualism, as well as her "bad," cigarette-smoking, gin-drinking reputation repels people, and her sickness only intensifies that feeling of repulsion. People gossip about Shug ("slut, hussy, heifer") and turn their backs on her and her "nasty woman disease." This sordid image of Shug is a shocking antithesis of what Celie and Mr. _____ have given us to believe was the "real," the glamorous Shug Avery.

Five days after Mr. _____ hears about Shug's being sick, and hears her being belittled and damned in church, he returns with her in the back of his wagon. We realize that Mr. _____ may be unfeeling and mean toward Celie, but that he deeply cares for Shug. Shug is "family" to him; he and Shug have three children together. (He and Celie have none.) In fact, note that Mr. _____ immediately tells Harpo that Shug (and not Annie Julia) should have been Harpo's mother.

As for Shug, the first thing we read about the Queen Honeybee's arrival is Celie's sight of "one of her foots . . . poking out" of the wagon. This is clearly *not* the entrance of a "queen." Yet, despite the fact that Shug looks literally ill to Celie, Shug looks dazzlingly dressed for the occasion. In contrast, as we read Celie's description of Shug, we get a completely different picture of her. She seems to be something that has already passed over to the next world and returned. She staggers toward Celie with a caked, yellowed powdered black face smeared with red rouge, her chest heaving with black beads, chicken hawk feathers curving down one cheek, and clutching a snakeskin bag. To Celie, Shug may be ill, but she still seems to be a beautiful creature, "so stylish it like the trees all round the house draw themself up tall for a better look." To us, in contrast, Shug seems to be deteriorating, going downhill fast in body and soul.

Shug's body may be sick, but we soon see that her spirit is clearly intact; in fact, her first words to Celie are loud, cackling, and cruel—particularly when we consider how much Celie reveres this woman. "You sure *is* ugly," Shug tells Celie, which is probably the most dramatically reinforced proof that Celie has ever had of her own

ugliness. She remembers that Fonso called her ugly, but here, Shug
proclaims that Celie sure *is* ugly.

The pain of hearing Shug confirm Celie's ugliness, however, isn't
as painful to Celie as is the fact that Celie can't tell Shug to come in;
she doesn't feel free to offer to take care of Shug. Celie doesn't feel
that she has the right to offer help – "It not my house." Celie feels like
Mr. _____'s slave; she doesn't even feel as though she is permitted
to speak unless given permission to do so by Mr. _____. And from
what Celie tells God, regarding Shug's statement that Celie sure is ugly,
we gather that Mr. _____ has already told Shug that Celie is ugly,
and that Shug had doubted that Celie really could be as ugly as
Mr. _____ said she was. Now that Shug sees Celie, she is ready
to agree with Mr. _____: Celie sure *is* ugly.

While Shug recovers at Mr. _____'s house, there are several
matters that one should consider.

First, realize how Celie loves Shug – first, she loves her as one
human being might love another, and second, she loves her as a Christian might love another human being. When Mr. _____ gives Shug
to Celie to care for, it is no chore for Celie. Instead, it is a source of
pleasure and excitement. Celie innocently looks at Shug and confesses
to God that she thought she had been turned "into a man." Shug's naked
body is that exciting to Celie.

At the same time, in a spiritual sense, Celie feels as though she
is performing a sacred rite when she is bathing Shug's naked body.
This two-edged feeling is in keeping with Celie's attitude toward Shug
and toward herself – both with Celie's idea of herself as a lowly servant
(waiting on Shug the queen), while in a spiritual sense, Celie feels
as though she is performing God's work. By her own admission, she
says that when she is washing Shug, "It feel like I'm praying."

Also, be aware that although Celie is a good Christian woman,
she is absolutely fascinated by the "evil" that she feels is deeply rooted
inside Shug. Shug yells and shouts and curses and is "more evil than
[Celie's] mother," but Celie is not repulsed. She remains fixated on
the worldly, wicked, and wondrous Shug Avery.

Later, when Shug seems to be recovering, she begins to hum a
tune while Celie is tending to her. The tune is a blues song, and Celie
is none too happy to hear her humming a blues song, but Shug's
humming this song is a sign for us that Shug is coming to life again.
Shug, too, realizes what is happening, and she gives all the credit to

Celie. Celie may not be pleased to hear the "low down dirty" blues song, but she must feel deeply satisfied when Shug tells her that the music is something which Celie "scratched out" of Shug's head. This is the first appreciative remark that Shug has shared with Celie.

In fact, Shug's brusque veneer begins to dissolve the more she is around Celie. She even asks Celie not to call her "Ma'm"; Shug realizes that they not only share Mr. _____, but that both of them are mothers without their children. The absence of their children and the absence of Mr. _____ when they are together allow them to care for one another.

As further proof that Celie continues to have a deep affection for Shug, despite Shug's vicious tongue and her loose ways, note that Celie hopes someday to fasten some of Shug's hair into her own hair, much as she was anxious earlier to sew a quilt together with Sofia's help (Letter 21). Celie thinks that every inch of Shug is precious. Her caring for Shug is much like taking care of the babies whom she never had a chance to rear. Remember, too, that with Mr. _____'s daughters' hair (Letter 9), Celie had little patience, but here, with Shug's hair, she is extremely careful to be gentle.

Like Celie, Albert adores Shug. Even Celie is aware of this. She knows that Mr. _____ and Shug know each other's secrets. Shug knows Mr. _____'s first name, Albert, and calls him by it. This indicates that they are equals in their relationship, or even perhaps that Shug has the upper hand. It is an altogether different set up than what Albert shares with Celie.

However, Albert is not as mean to Celie now that the softening element of Shug is in the house. For the first time, he shows a tiny bit of concern for Celie's feelings—something he has never done before. He wants to know if Celie minds if Shug stays in the house; he wants to know how Celie feels about Shug's being there. Celie is stunned at his concern for her, Celie, and she is more than a little puzzled at the depth of his concern for Shug. She sees his eyes mist over as he tells Celie that "Nobody fight for Shug." Shug brings out both emotion and sensitivity within Albert. But not enough. Albert doesn't realize that no one fights for Celie.

The bond between Celie and Albert is strengthened when Albert's father arrives and expresses disgust that Albert has taken the diseased and dark-skinned Shug into his home. Secretly, Celie spits into the man's glass of water and tells God that "This is the closest us [she and

Albert] ever felt." And all because of Shug Avery. Even Albert's brother Tobias comes to assess the situation.

In these scenes, you should be aware that neither Albert's father nor Tobias came to "inspect" Celie, Albert's legal wife. Instead, Albert's sisters, Kate and Carrie, came to inspect Celie's housekeeping. The sexual division, the sexist dimension of this society, is distinct. Women come to evaluate a wife and her work. Men come to question another man's judgment, particularly when a "trifling" love relationship might socially and financially destroy a man. The narrow sexist dimensions of the status quo society of Albert, his family, and Celie stand in stark contrast to the brassy, liberated world of the recovering Shug Avery.

## Letters 28–32

For the most part, these letters concern Harpo's aching unhappiness because of the fact that the only role model he has for being a husband and a man is that of his indolent father, Albert. Unfortunately, Harpo thinks that he himself is a failure – simply because he can't beat Sofia, like Albert beats Celie. Harpo doesn't realize that his role model is wrong – not Harpo himself – and as long as Harpo is married to Sofia, he will never be able to treat her as Albert treats Celie. Sofia is a big woman; she won't stand for it.

For that reason, then, Harpo tries unconsciously to be big – big and strong and powerful – like Sofia. But that too fails; all he gets is fat. He becomes the butt of many jokes and gets such a pot belly that he looks pregnant. Yet, in his case, he is not pregnant with anything positive; he is bloated with confusion and resentment and self-pity.

Harpo doesn't realize that he is far luckier than his father. He and Sofia truly love one another – despite their constant fighting. Between Albert and Celie, there is no emotion. Therefore, in a marriage like Harpo and Sofia's, where there is love, there is also room for variation in roles. This is why Harpo and Sofia are able to divide the cooking and the cleaning. In a loveless marriage, such as Albert and Celie have, there is no room for variation. Celie must do what she is told, and Albert does whatever *he* wants.

Celie tries to explain to Harpo that Albert and Shug are in love and that their relationship works because of their love for one another, but Celie points out that they are not married. A wife and a mistress always have different duties. Harpo still doesn't understand.

Sofia realizes that life with Harpo is a dead-end situation; she needs a vacation. Old indolent Albert, on the other hand, doesn't have to go away to restore his soul because Shug is with him. Because Shug is his mistress and because he loves her, he can allow himself the freedom to "reach over and pick something out her hair." Harpo cannot do this with Sofia because he still thinks that, somehow, he must be dominant and exhibit power and authority.

Harpo is crying as Sofia leaves, wiping his eyes with a baby diaper. Sofia's sisters have rescued her. Harpo has no brothers to rescue him.

Celie, remember, once tried to rescue Nettie when Nettie fled from Fonso and came to live with Celie. But eventually, Nettie had to flee from Albert's lust and brutality. At present, Nettie is only a precious, painful memory to Celie. Neither one of them can rescue the other. In childhood, each had been a haven for the other. No longer.

Sofia, Celie realizes, is lucky to have her sisters. And perhaps that is why Celie gives Sofia the quilt which they made together, the "Sister's Choice" quilt. It is Celie's choice to give it to Sofia. Rarely does Celie have a choice about anything. Once, she planned to give the quilt to Shug if it were perfect, or keep it herself if it were imperfect. At the critical moment of choice, however, neither perfect nor imperfect makes any difference. What makes the difference is that Celie *chooses* to make Sofia even more of a sister and so, spontaneously, she gives her the quilt out of love and sisterhood.

## Letters 33–35

These letters are primarily concerned with Celie's emotional, physical, and geographical isolation and now – because of Shug Avery – these letters focus on Celie's "awakening" from her isolation. This awakening first begins in Harpo's jukejoint. Shug is so grateful that Celie has nursed her back to health that she sings "Miss Celie's Song" to her, and Celie's heart immediately begins to cramp. In other words, Celie's heart begins to come to life again. No one has ever done anything so special for Celie since years ago, since Celie and Nettie were children.

Since then, Celie has been isolated from the external world. The word "plantation" (on Harpo's handbills) appears for the first time in the novel; Celie has been living on a plantation all her life and doesn't even know it. Likewise, she has never heard of the diva of the blues, Bessie Smith. There is no radio or record player in Albert's house, and he doesn't allow Celie to go out to nightclubs. There is irony in the fact that Harpo sought to isolate himself even farther from the police by "secluding" his jukejoint off the road, because it is in this calculated seclusion that Celie begins to discover that she is of value — to herself and to Shug Avery. Shug's song affirms that Celie has worth, and this truth is almost more than Celie can believe.

One might think that Shug would dedicate her song to Mr. _____, to Albert, since he was the one who came and got her and arranged for her to be nursed back to life, but Shug doesn't do the "expected." She gives credit where it is due — to Celie. Shug is an intense, soulful woman full of fire and candor, and she knows whom to appreciate. Once more, Harpo is puzzled. He realizes that Shug does what she wants to do and that she "forgit about polite."

In these letters, we see two parallel sequences of "awakening." Earlier, Celie helped Shug awaken to life again, and now, Celie helps transform the naked woman whom she bathed to be "clothed" again in her "stage self," the Queen Honeybee. This takes some time because a good deal of time has elapsed, and Shug's hair is considerably longer, and pressing her hair is done by using a very hot iron comb. This process is also called "straightening" because it removes the kinky curls from black hair.

Besides Shug's awakening to new life, there is also, as we mentioned earlier, Celie's awakening to a sense of herself. This is the first time since Nettie left that Celie has felt "special" and loved, and she has Shug to thank for it. Shug is the source of Celie's happiness. It is significant that Shug waits until she is on stage to thank Celie. She wants everyone to know. She values Celie that much.

Shug has recovered, but she stays on at Albert's in order to protect Celie from Albert's beatings, and she vows not to leave "until I know Albert won't even think about beating you." The two women share a long embrace that ends in a kiss, bonding their relationship.

In order for Celie to grow as a woman, it is necessary for her to learn who she is — emotionally and physically. And it is at this point that some readers flinch as they read about Shug's showing Celie how to masturbate — a clinical verb with ugly connotations. What Shug is really doing, however, is not ugly; it is beautiful. Shug is teaching Celie how to give herself pleasure, how to make herself feel good. One can never love another person or another body until one has learned to love oneself and one's own body. A person must know what feels good sexually and be able to tell one's partner.

Celie has had two children, but she knows little about her own body. Shug's response to Celie's ignorance is precisely on-target: "Why Miss Celie you still a virgin." That is, Celie has never experienced orgasm or physical pleasure, or even emotional pleasure when she has had sex. Sex, to Shug, is synonymous with delicious pleasure, and if Celie is ignorant of that pleasure, then she is still a virgin to the world of sexuality.

Celie, of course, doesn't know anything about her button of a clitoris and is very naturally confused when she feels shivering, hot pulsing waves of sexual excitement crashing within herself. She is so used to pain that pain seems "normal." She feels guilty about discovering her pleasure center, and it will be a while before she feels free enough to make herself feel good. Shug, remember, is still sleeping with Albert. Celie is sleeping alone. Certainly, Celie could masturbate and bring pleasure to herself, but for the present, she cannot. Celie would like to tell Shug to stop sleeping with Albert, but because she cannot, she masturbates, as Shug has taught her to, but with no pleasure. She cries herself to sleep.

## Letters 36–40

One of the ways to approach this particular series of letters lies in the idea of "strength"—that is, what does "strong" mean? Does it mean physical might? The evidence in this novel seems to indicate that black men use physical might in order to keep their wives in their place—just as white men have used physical might to keep the black man in his place. Certainly, Sofia tends to solve all her problems with physical violence. She learned a long time ago that you have to fight: "All my life I had to fight," she told Celie in Letter 21.

However, in these letters, we see something emerging which is even stronger than physical might. It is the strength of bonding between black blood-sisters and black friend-sisters. Bonding joins these different black women together just as scraps of cloth are joined together to form a new, strong whole creation—a quilt, a central metaphor in Letter 40 and throughout the novel.

To begin with, we are introduced to a man who looks like a professional "strong man." To Celie, he is "Prizefighter," so we assume for the sake of the story that he is one. Prizefighter's name is Henry "Buster" Broadax; he is Sofia's new man. Unlike Harpo, Buster feels no need to beat Sofia into submission since he won her admiration by fighting in the ring. This recognized strong man is not a violent man, however, except professionally. Privately, Buster is a gentleman, explaining that his job is "to love [Sofia] and take her where she want to go."

Sofia, on the other hand, even though she is a mother with six children, always uses violence to solve her problems. Violence is the only weapon that Sofia has against black men and white society. In fact, Letter 36 is proof that Sofia is not above slugging two teeth out of a black sister if that woman is dumb enough to strike out and slap Sofia.

Harpo's mistress, Squeak, ventures into the world of violence for the first time and tangles with the wrong woman. Normally, Squeak is passive—"Like me," Celie says, and we realize that Squeak did not strike out stupidly at Sofia. Squeak was trying to defend her place in Harpo's life and her place in Harpo's home, especially after she heard Harpo tell Sofia that his house, the jukejoint, was still Sofia's house.

In an almost parallel situation, Sofia slugs the white mayor, who is trying to patronize Sofia and take her out of her own home in an effort to try and put her in his wife's kitchen. Sofia, like Squeak, is not going to passively allow another woman to take her away from territory that is hers. But in the case of the mayor, Sofia's violence encounters even a stronger violence than Sofia's—that is, the violence of the white police. Sofia is overpowered and is sentenced to twelve years in prison. Ironically, Sofia's strongman boyfriend, "Buster," cannot save the woman he loves from a force more powerful even than violence—that is, he cannot save Sofia from the iron fist of racism.

Had Sofia not fought back at the whites, however, she still would have been punished because she cursed the mayor's wife, and had she not fought back, she would have always wished she had. There was no way that Sofia could keep her dignity and not offend the mayor and his wife. Ultimately, the whites gave Sofia no choice.

We realize anew that there is no justice for blacks in the white system of "law and justice," and yet, despite those odds, Squeak, Shug, Celie, and Odessa (Sofia's sister) make plans to try and defy "the system." By using cunning and deviousness, they hope to keep Sofia from serving twelve years in a prison that is already making her a broken and helpless emotional and psychological cripple.

Just as Albert and Celie earlier befriended Shug from the town gossips, now Shug, Celie, Squeak, and Odessa mean to defend Sofia. These women have witnessed and suffered great pain through years of degrading injustice in their own lives, but they have been able, somehow, to cope with it, and now they realize that Sofia can no longer cope by herself. Celie says, "When I see Sofia, I don't know why she still alive." Sofia's spirit has been broken by the whites. It is almost miracle-like that she manages to stay alive. Touchingly, and yet humorously, Sofia tells Celie that the only way that she survives is by acting "like I'm you. I jump right up and do just what they say." Sofia endures—but just barely. She has become a cipher.

It is totally unexpected that Squeak—Little Miss Mouse—is chosen to be the strongest link in the sisterhood of strength and defiance. Squeak is chosen to be the mediator between the black woman Sofia and the white man who represents Prison. For that reason, perhaps, Walker chooses to have Squeak described as "yellowish." Squeak is half-white and half-black, meaning that she has milky skin. Moreover, Squeak admits reluctantly that she is related to the white prison warden. Racially, Squeak is a link between the two races. Now, that "link" between the two races will be used, hopefully, to free Sofia from her prison sentence.

Squeak agrees to go to her white uncle and plead for Sofia, the woman whose children she has been a stepmother to during Sofia's term in prison. Squeak's role as a mediator demands unusual strength, but Celie recognizes the fierce spirit that is alive and strong within the tiny-voiced, diminutive Squeak. "She carry on," says Celie, "Hair a little stringy, slip show, but she carry on." The power of racism is strong enough to unite (1) Squeak and Sofia, these two women whom we saw fighting between themselves not long ago, as well as unite (2) the dramatically dissimilar Celie and Shug and Odessa.

Letter 40 describes the women's plan: they intend to dress up Squeak like a white woman. This in itself shows us how far the women are willing to go in order to try and manipulate the dominating white power structure. They know that the odds aren't good, but they have hope.

Squeak is wearing a dress, and although it is patched, it is starched and ironed, and, in addition, Squeak has on high heels and a hat and carries a quilt-design purse and a Bible—a bizarre combination, certainly, almost crazy-quiltlike, but remember that the image of a quilt is one of the metaphorical devices that unifies the fabric of this novel.

The grease that the women wash out of Squeak's hair in order to make her look more persuasive is a petroleum jelly-based moisturizer used to keep Squeak's hair soft. It is applied to soften her hair, but it is shampooed out when she is about to pay her visit to jail because of its smell. It becomes rancid when left in too long. Squeak must appear to be a proper, humble black woman, but one with enough "style" to dress like a white woman. The smell of hair grease wouldn't help her in her charade.

Squeak no doubt resembles on the surface what a white woman in advertisements looks like to Shug and Celie and Odessa. But with God and luck and Squeak's "white" accessories, the women's plan might just work.

One of the central things that you should be aware of in this scene is Walker's focus on the women's preparation for their undertaking. They know that not only is Squeak's appearance important, but that her performance is important also. The women are trying to out-think the white man. They are hoping that he will be naive enough to believe that a black woman is happier in prison than she would be in the kitchen of a white woman. Therefore, using Brer Rabbit psychology, they hope to convince the white man if he *really* wants to punish Sofia, he would take her out of prison and make her work for a white woman. Sofia's boldness, they hope he will remember, confirms this fact. Sadly, however, the real truth of the matter is this: Sofia cannot truly be happy in any place that confines her.

The mention of Uncle Tom in this letter is intentional. In literature, Uncle Tom was a clever and intelligent slave who was able to help his people. Harriet Beecher Stowe immortalized him in her novel *Uncle Tom's Cabin*. Since then, however, the term "Tomming" has come to mean the overly polite actions of a fawning and flattering black person who is trying to win favor with a white person, or escape punishment. It is ironic that Shug tells Squeak to be sure and tell the warden that she, Squeak, thinks that "justice ought to be done." When did a black man or woman, in the time frame of this novel, ever receive justice?

Again, note that one of the keys to this letter lies in the motif of quilts and patches. Both quilts and patches are symbolic of how the black women in this novel, as well as all black people whose families have been torn to scraps by the white man, must unite to fight against the whites. Just as pieces of separate garments are joined together and used to make a warm and enduring patchwork quilt, a sense of strong, patchwork unity can strengthen the women as they attempt to try and save Sofia.

## Letters 41 & 42

After Squeak returns, she and Celie have something in common: they both have been raped by a relative. The white warden, of course, doesn't think that it was wrong to rape his niece – Squeak is black. In the American South, there is an unwritten law that if a person has any black blood at all in him or her, even the most miniscule amount, then that person is black – in other words, a non-person. This "law" came about, among other things, because of the greed of white slaveowners who wanted to have the most slaves. Accordingly, if a child had a white father and a black slave mother, the child was black and a slave.

Shug's impatient words to Squeak, when Squeak resists describing how she was raped, are significant: "If you can't tell us, who you gon tell, God?" The very first words of this novel, remember, were: "You better not never tell nobody but God"; Squeak then decides to tell her friends that she was raped. Celie, of course, decided to tell God; she had no friends to tell. Celie's rape is worse, ultimately, because as far as she knows, she was raped by her father, and he violated not only Celie, but he violated the sacredness and the unity of the family.

Squeak's suffering makes her stronger, and she demands that Harpo call her by her real name as Celie suggested earlier, in Letter 37. Squeak has earned the right to be called by her real name, Mary Agnes. In addition, she begins composing her own blues songs and stops singing Shug's songs. Tellingly, her songs are reflective; she questions, in particular, the double standard concerning color preference among black people.

Harpo's anger over Squeak's rape is impotent, as always. He talks about violence and revolution as a means of bringing about liberation and justice, saying, "I ought to go back out there with guns, maybe set fire to the place, burn the crackers [poor white Southerners] up." But Harpo only *talks* about his anger; he does not act on it. In contrast, the women act on their anger and frustration, and as we shall see later, they are successful in extricating Sofia from prison.

## Letters 43–45

These letters are structured with irony. It is painfully ironic that

Sofia leaves prison only to become the one thing that she absolutely refused to become: a white woman's maid. And the irony is compounded by the fact that she must watch over Miss Millie's children and not her own. Prison may have been hard on Sofia, but, ironically, being a "maid" is far harder on Sofia, psychologically. Isolation in prison gave Sofia enough time to reflect on her situation; she has been a victim of both racism and sexism. Her life at present is a kind of non-life. She has looked at the abyss of her future, and like one of Camus' characters, she has seen the absurdity of living, even though she does continue to live. She knows that she and Miss Millie can never have the kind of relationship that two women should have; they can have a relationship based only on differences and protocol – the antithesis of Sofia's sisterhood with Celie, Squeak, and Odessa.

The white community refers to Sofia, a woman with six children, as a "girl." Yet, Sofia realizes ironically how "girl-like" and ignorant Miss Millie is, while, at the same time, Sofia has to act *as if* Miss Millie were superior. Camus' world of the absurd is lived in, day-to-day, as if rules, customs, and observances mattered – while knowing, at the same time, how hollow they are. Sofia knows how thoroughly immersed in racism Miss Millie is, and she also knows how terribly deluded the "do-good" white woman is. It is little wonder that Sofia is relieved and happy to admit that she is glad that she is "not white."

As a small footnote, you should be aware that ever since Letter 36, we have seen the development of cars and their being integrated into the daily lives of rural blacks. Sofia's prizefighter has a car, and, of course, Miss Millie has one. Shug has a fancy, queenly dark blue Packard for herself and Grady. These cars are a symbol of mobility as well as a symbol of progress. The wagons of the early letters seem to be gone. The years are rolling by, and Celie, whom we met at fourteen, is now approaching middle-age.

## Letters 46–48

The reappearance of Shug, now with a husband, reawakens Celie's interest in herself. Unlike the years when she didn't mind being plain and ragged (because "it bees that way sometimes"), Celie now minds a lot. Shug is back, and Shug has reawakened Celie's sense of values. Now, however, the sight of Shug makes Celie feel plain and insignificant once again. Celie is jealous of Grady; she doesn't want to share Shug with such an unworthy man – especially with a man who calls

Shug "Mamma." Clearly, Shug dominates Grady; even Celie realizes this.

Shug, in turn, realizes that Albert still treats Celie demeaningly, and she is loud about the value that she puts on Celie. She tells Celie that if Celie were her wife, "I'd cover you up with kisses stead of licks." Shug knows now that no matter how seemingly kind Albert was to her when she was ill, he is ultimately incapable of showing affection and deep appreciation. To Albert's credit, we should be aware that he does try to stimulate Celie sexually, but fails. His doing so, however, seems more of an effort to please Shug than it does to please Celie.

Therefore, Celie has still not experienced sexual orgasm. But she has "awakened" to the distinction between rough sex and making love. She knows that rough, ramming sex is not love; rape of one's wife is barbaric and, in contrast, making love is pure and natural and tender. But Celie has never yet made love to a man.

Now that Celie has shed her stoic, protective husk, she can admit and even indulge in a little self-pity. She tells Shug that nobody ever loved her. This is not wholly true. Nettie loved Celie; she still does. But no one has ever "made love" to Celie—not in the sense that a physical lover would make love to her. Therefore, Shug tells Celie that she loves Celie, and their passionate kissing and fondling is so intense that it overwhelms Celie. She describes feeling as though she were a "little lost baby." Celie makes love for the first time (Letter 47); she is no longer a virgin.

Shug, the flashy blues singer whom some people think of as shallow and immoral, is a strong, positive character in this novel. She gives great value to Celie's life, and, likewise, she does a similar thing for Squeak. She encourages Squeak to sing, despite Harpo's old-fashioned notion that "good" women don't sing in jukejoints. Not surprisingly, Shug gets her way, and Squeak realizes that she, Mary Agnes, can sing.

## Letters 49–51

These three letters are filled to the brim with joy and hope and promise. Celie tells God that she finally holds a letter from Nettie. Nettie's letter with the funny-looking stamps is proof that not only is Nettie alive, but that Celie's babies—Olivia and Adam—are also alive and are "coming home before the end of another year." Celie's joy, you should note, is doubled because she has someone to share it with: Shug.

We realize that Nettie, although she is now a missionary, is not and never was as naive as Celie was. She is aware that Albert has probably been hiding her letters from Celie, but she counts on the sentiment associated with Christmas and Easter to perhaps soften his fierce resolve to punish both her and Celie by keeping her letters from Celie.

How do we know that Albert has been deliberately cruel and vindictive for all these years? From two things that Celie says, and Celie doesn't lie. Initially, she tells Shug that Albert couldn't have kept Nettie's letters from her because he knew that Nettie "mean everything in the world to me." But later, she tells God that she finds the letters in Albert's trunk, and "everything that mean something to Albert go in his trunk." Clearly, Albert has structured his life around deliberately punishing both Nettie *and* Celie – for Nettie's rebuff long ago and for Celie's not being either Nettie or Shug.

Celie's normally gentle character is transformed immediately. Even she herself realizes that she's acting "just like Sofia," muttering and "crazy for Mr. _____'s blood." And now that Celie is strong enough to listen to Shug's evaluation of Mr. _____, Shug explains that Albert wasn't always as mean and callous as he has been to Celie, but that he used to dance, laugh, and make her feel great. Shug's affair with Albert "had to be good," Shug explains, or otherwise she could never have loved him. Albert was Shug's first source of unlimited affection; she was reared by a reserved mother and an inhibited father. Shug was hurt when Albert married Annie Julia – and that was part of the reason why Shug treated Celie "so mean. Like you was a servant." It was after Annie Julia's death that Albert changed.

Now that Celie knows about Shug's relationship with Albert, and Shug knows about Celie's background of rape and mistreatment, the two women become even closer, especially so since Shug found one of Nettie's letters in the mailbox and, along with Celie, she was determined to find the rest of Nettie's letters.

Celie is reunited with Nettie, even though they are continents apart. The person who meant more to her than anyone else in the world is alive. Despite the fact that Celie never received any letters from Nettie, she never stopped loving her and never became bitter about the fact that she never received any letters. In fact, Celie's constant love for Nettie has been a source of sustaining strength for her, and now that Nettie is alive, Celie's self-confidence becomes so strong that she will frighten the men who have made her cower for so long. Celie takes the strength of Sofia, the spunk and sass of Shug, and she draws on her own awakened, rightful sense of vengeance to emerge a solid, independent, courageous, and admired woman.

## Letters 52–58

The notion of "chance" plays a major role in this novel; already we have seen that Fonso's chance perversion of values caused Celie, and not Nettie, to be married to Albert. But Albert's mistress was (by chance) Shug Avery, who was, first, responsible for slowly instilling in Celie a sense of self-worth, and she was, second, responsible for intercepting one of Nettie's letters and helping Celie find the rest of her letters. There is so much almost pre-determined mean and brutal behavior and suffering in this novel that chance, being an antithetical element for good, seems to be drawn by some unnamed natural force to help counter the immense weight of all of the injustice and unhappiness in Celie's life.

Likewise, in a parallel way, we see that chance also enters into Nettie's life. By chance, Nettie is able to find Celie and Albert when she runs away from Fonso's brutal sexual attacks; later, when she is confronted by Albert, she is able to escape only, we gather, by chance. Then, by chance, Nettie is pointed in the direction of Samuel and Corrine's house, a couple who, by chance, bought both of Celie's babies. By chance, also, both Celie and Nettie are intuitive; like Celie, Nettie immediately recognizes Corrine's babies as being Celie's. Likewise, when Nettie sees Sofia and Miss Millie, by chance, Nettie perceives immediately that Sofia is not maid material. In addition, it is by chance that one of the missionaries can't go to Africa, and so there is a free ticket available for Nettie to go along and continue to look after Celie's children.

Besides the theme of chance, this set of letters is also infused with Nettie's hopeful, fighting spirit and her joy of learning. Nettie fought against Fonso's advances and escaped; then she fought against Albert's advances and escaped; now, despite Albert's threats, she continues to write to Celie, and her first message to Celie is: *fight!* Defying all the odds, Nettie plunges forward, fighting, into life. She plans to do missionary work despite the fact that she's very young and despite the fact that the white men "in charge" at the Missionary Society of New York are discouraging. Nettie believes that, with God, all things are possible. A key phrase in one of these letters to Celie is: "if you believe. . . ." Nettie's faith never wavers, and because of that, she grows stronger and stronger.

Nettie is obviously a born teacher; we saw her teaching Celie earlier, she teaches in Africa, and here in her letters to Celie, she continues to do so. She tells Celie about all the marvelous insights that she has had into their black heritage.

For example, (1) it was Africans (and not white men) who sold blacks into slavery; (2) Jesus had lamb's wool-like hair (i.e., kinky); (3) the Africans had, at one time, a more advanced civilization than the Europeans had at a comparable period; (4) truly black – dazzlingly *blue*black – Africans have made Nettie admire anew her black skin and her black race; and (5) Nettie vividly describes the profoundly moving emotion which she felt on seeing the African coast for the first time.

We read Nettie's letters and realize that for the first time, Nettie has experienced great pride in being a black woman. She is delighted to learn that her people are beautiful and diverse. She is joyous because she now knows that she is a part of something greater than she ever imagined: Africa. She is ready to help "uplift black people everywhere."

Nettie is, as we shall continue to see, a part of history. Marcus Garvey, a Jamaican black, immigrated to New York in the late 1930s. He was the founder of black nationalism and pan-Africanism; he wanted blacks to go back to Africa and create a powerful empire. His movement, often called Garveyism, was especially popular in Harlem, the black section of New York. Nettie's prose reflects some of his ideology. "We and the Africans will be working for a common goal: the uplift of black people everywhere." Harlem opens Nettie's eyes to possibility. Nettie has always believed in the notion of possibility, but now the word takes on enormous importance in terms of black people on two continents.

## Letters 59–61

Only one matter deeply worries Celie now – the matter of incest; she believes that her own father is the father of her two babies. According to folklore, Adam and Olivia may grow up to be retarded.

This fear will be alleviated eventually, but because Celie can now hope to reclaim her babies someday, the possibility of brain-damaged children preys on her hopes for a perfect, joyous reunion with Nettie, Adam, and Olivia.

At this point, Celie considers Olivia and Adam to be her and Nettie's children. "Her and me and our two children," she says. Celie hasn't taken time to reflect on the fact that she can't suddenly claim the children as hers. Even they consider themselves to be Samuel and Corrine's children.

In the meantime, we return to Celie's transformation from a meek, submissive woman into a woman filled with fury. The cause for the transformation, of course, is found in Nettie's letters to Celie. Celie, you should realize, was not able to read through her sister's letters as quickly and as comprehensively as we can. Nettie's letters are unusually lucid to us, but Celie and Shug have trouble with Nettie's vocabulary. It would have been unrealistic to expect Celie and Shug to understand everything that Nettie wrote about. But what the two women can't understand literally, they understand emotionally because Nettie's letters are powerfully written. Celie and Shug understand what Nettie *means*. They understand, most of all, that Albert deliberately chose to sever Celie from the one human being in the world whom she loved most.

Celie's outrage is immediate—and rightfully justified. For all these years, Albert has lived with festering hate and vengeance in his heart, and he has beat Celie for no reason—other than the fact that Celie wasn't Nettie or Shug. No wonder Celie is now ready to kill him. She has the certain knowledge of Albert's theft and concealment, as well as a brand-new feeling of power. Celie is filled with a sense of righteous vengeance, and she wants to act—immediately and violently.

Ironically, it is Shug, the "notorious," sinful woman, who reminds Celie of the biblical commandment "Thou Shalt Not Kill." And it is Shug who tells Celie, in essence, that she must rise above the black male code of rage and headstrong brutality. Celie, Shug insists, is better than the black men who have physically abused her for so long. Celie is "somebody" now, and she is especially somebody to Nettie. Celie owes it to Nettie to act maturely with this new and certain knowledge of Albert's mean-spirited, long-lasting vindictiveness.

Therefore, Celie's new strength begins to articulate itself in more peaceful ways; she orders Shug to tell Albert to start sleeping alone.

Shug complies and begins sleeping with a new, angry and proud black woman named Celie.

Shug is proud of Celie and wants to make her comfortable, less frustrated in her new role. For that reason, Shug decides to make Celie a pair of pants. Initially, Celie objects, but Shug explains that Celie will have more freedom of movement, literally, if she doesn't wear dresses. On a symbolic level, of course, Shug has decided to introduce Celie to options and practicality. There is no reason for Celie to be confined in a dress (a symbol of female oppression) when she can explore the possibilities that exist for a person who wears pants. Remember that in Letter 28, Celie watched Sofia – strong in her role as an independent-minded woman, dragging a ladder and "wearing a old pair of Harpo pants." In addition, making pants with Shug is similar to Sofia's and Celie's joint efforts in making the "Sister's Choice" quilt.

Returning to the matter of Nettie's letters, Nettie continues to be Celie's teacher, anxious to share with Celie some comparisons that she has made between black Africans and black Americans. The Olinka people have never seen black Americans. To them, missionaries have come mostly from the white European world. Remember that in this regard, black Americans are at least a dozen generations removed from Africa, but there is still a link. The two black peoples have the same common ancestors and the same dark skin.

At one point, Joseph, the spokesman for the Olinka, says poignantly:

> The white missionary before you would not let us have this ceremony. But Olinka like it very much. We know a roofleaf is not Jesus Christ, but in its own humble way, is it not God?

Joseph's intuitive knowledge about the Christian religion is strong and intense. Joseph has grasped the central Christian tenet that God is omnipresent and can therefore only be represented symbolically. A cross is no better than a roofleaf. The wood of the cross was sacred to early Christians, just as a roofleaf is sacred to the Olinka people. Joseph also has made the distinction between Jesus Christ and God. He knows that Jesus Christ is the "person" of the Holy Trinity and that God is not only the father, but the creator. God made the roofleaf, and it is therefore part of him.

The origins of modern-day American soul food are also of interest in Nettie's letters. Soul food, we discover, originally came from West Africa, and later, during the era of slavery, the slaves were given the scraps of the butchered pig – that is, the feet, the neck, and the back. Slave owners also gave them overly ripe tomatoes. They added sugar and vinegar to the tomatoes and barbecued the pork. This cooking practice of barbecuing, so familiar in America, is like the open pit roasting and flaming and flavoring that goes on in West African villages. Nettie had probably never thought of any place but the South as being the original source of barbecuing. "Yes," she says, "a barbecue. They remind me of folks at home!"

You might also enjoy noticing something else in this letter that could easily be overlooked. Remember that after the dedication page in the novel, there are the words, "Show me how to do like you, Show me how to do it." This is quoted from blind musician Stevie Wonder's 1980 album, *Hotter than July*. The song is "Do I Do." It is about a young boy burning with the desire to sing and dance on stage at a talent show. His mother prohibits him, but he goes and does a smashing performance. The message of the song is that performing is learning. Walker has placed the words "Hotter than July" in Letter 61. A few sentences prior, Celie writes, "What they look like, I wonder." Seemingly, Walker is inserting here her appreciation of Stevie Wonder and his music.

## Letters 62–67

One of the themes running throughout *The Color Purple* concerns sex roles. Whether the problem of sex roles focuses on Harpo and Sofia, or on Albert and Celie, or on Grady and Shug, there is always a clear-cut sexual division of labor, and tensions usually arise when one half of the couple doesn't like his or her "role," or duties. Likewise, in Africa, tensions arise from very similar problems concerning sex roles.

Nettie, for example, is no one's wife; she is "married" to her missionary work. The Olinka look askance at unwed women. They hold marriage between two people to be the be-all and end-all purpose of a woman's life. To them, Nettie is a non-person. When she and Samuel, Corrine, and the babies arrived, the Olinka wanted to know if she were Samuel's second wife. Had she been, they would have held her in esteem. Since she was not, they think of her as having little status.

Catherine, an Olinka woman, tells Nettie, "You are not much. The missionary's drudge." Yet, in spite of being judged to be a social inferior, Nettie has a good appreciation and respect for herself. "I am something," she writes Celie—a statement that, until now, we can't imagine Celie ever saying about herself.

Nettie wants to understand the Olinka; she does not want to offend them by defying their "system," so she doesn't rebel as Shug might have in a similar situation. Instead, she keeps quiet, very much like Celie, but unlike Celie, Nettie has a sense of deep respect for herself which she never loses.

Nettie's niece, Olivia, on the other hand, understands that the Olinka's withholding education from females is a means of suppression not unlike white Americans keeping the blacks from learning. Ignorance keeps Olinka women and American blacks limited. The Olinka are puzzled by Olivia's independence. They can interpret Olivia's intelligence as a sign that she might someday marry a chief, but they cannot envision the possibility that Olivia might someday attain importance in her own right.

In this context of women's suppression, it is just possible that Corrine could be pleased to be a sort of non-person as a wife and mother. Remember that she has tried to hide her children's origins. She does not want anyone to know that she is not her children's biological mother. We will discover eventually that she and Samuel suspect that Nettie might be the mother of Adam and Olivia; perhaps, then, this is Corrine's motivation for asking Nettie to call her "sister" and to call Samuel "brother." By suppressing not only herself, but her children's identities, as well as Nettie's identity, Corrine is preserving her own dignity, as well as maintaining the customary status quo for women and, especially, for missionary wives. Her rationalization, of course, is sound: how can she and Samuel hope to convert the Olinka if their Western values appear to be alien and unnatural?

If the Olinka are willing to make small social allowances for Olivia, though, the code is not so elastic concerning one of their own young women—Tashi, Olivia's best friend. The Olinka do not want Tashi to be exposed to the idea that perhaps she too might someday be more than a mere wife, even the wife of a chief. Nettie also wonders if Tashi should be exposed to the idea that women have worth; "Tashi," she says, "knows she is learning a way of life she will never live." Tashi's parents cling to their Olinka tradition because of their ethnocentrism – that is, the attitude that one's group is superior to another group. A daughter who is a misfit, harboring unnatural, "progressive" ideas can never be acceptable to them. They will never be despotic toward Nettie, whom they judge to be inferior because she is (1) an older, mature, unwed woman, and (2) an outsider. But toward their own people, the Olinka's ethnocentrism is so complete that it makes them not only want to keep Tashi from Nettie's house, but it compels them to want to change Olivia's values. They hope to teach young Olivia "what women are for."

Nettie compares the Olinka's ethnocentrism to that of white Southerners.

> I think Africans are very much like white people back
> home, in that they think they are the center of the
> universe and that everything is done for them.

Just as the slave traders arrived many years before and robbed Africa of its best people, the roadbuilders now rob the Africans of their homes and lands. The Olinka did not realize that the road was going to run through their village. They are symbolically blind to progress which they cannot halt. In Letter 64, they befriended the roadbuilders, who were their distant cousins. Much like the time when blacks sold their brothers into bondage to the white man, the roadbuilders are again executing the will of ruling whites.

Westernization, it is true, destroys frontier forests and sometimes it destroys villages, but it brings new hope for women. Girls now attend school. It took the advent of the road to force the Olinka to accept the fact that the real and powerful influence of the outside world could no longer be ignored. The Olinka can rage, but they cannot stop the onward, inward road of Westernization.

Nettie has so much self-assurance that Tashi's parents' outrage at Westernization does not make Nettie feel less of a person. She jokingly calls herself "a pitiful, castout woman who may perish during the rainy season." With humor like this, Nettie will endure. Clearly, she is a strong woman, and just as clearly, Olivia will be an even stronger woman.

The concept of a special sisterhood, or a female fellowship, that exists between women has run throughout the course of this novel. Celie and Nettie are an excellent example of this concept, as were

Sofia and Celie when they mended their differences and began to create a quilt together called "Sister's Choice" (Letter 28); they were living out Nettie's observation, a continent away, "It is in work that the women get to know and care about each other."

Focusing on Nettie's situation, while remembering Celie's situation, we could profitably imagine that Shug is Albert's "other wife," in the West African sense. Thus, Nettie's statement, "It was through work that Catherine became friends with her husband's other wives," can be understood more fully—thereby linking Nettie's exotic world far away with Celie's plain, country life in the South.

The two worlds, as dissimilar as we might think they are, have striking similarities. Shug and Celie (the mistress and wife of Albert) become friends, and almost immediately, neither woman will allow Albert into their circle. In fact, in Letter 64, Nettie writes about the male Olinka treatment of women, and we are vividly reminded of the way that Fonso treated Nettie and Celie's mother. Notice, too, that Nettie reports that Olinka husbands have "life and death power" over their wives; recall, as a parallel, that almost all of the Southern black men in this novel also attempt to have this fierce, brutal omnipotence over their wives. Their homes are *theirs;* a wife has claim on *nothing.* Fonso and Albert have made this edict savagely clear to Celie.

Nettie's relevation, in Letter 67, that Fonso is Nettie's and Celie's stepfather—and *not* their physical father—brings as much joy to Celie as did the discovery of Nettie's letters. In addition, we learn that Fonso was a friend of Samuel "long before [Samuel] found Christ." Nettie and Celie were born *before* Fonso married their widowed mother.

Irony again structures the lives of the two sisters who are continents apart. Both Samuel and Corrine thought that Nettie was the natural mother of Adam and Olivia, and just as Adam and Olivia think that Samuel is their natural father, Nettie and Celie thought Fonso was their natural father. Unlike Fonso, however, Samuel reared his children with patience, love, and Christian values—values which he learned after he was converted. Olivia and Adam will be disappointed to discover that Samuel is not their real father, but both Nettie and Celie are ecstatic and relieved to learn that the evil Fonso is only their stepfather. If Celie thought she knew perfect happiness when she discovered Nettie's letters, her emotions were pale compared to how she feels when she reads "Pa is not our pa!"

## Letters 68 & 69

The discovery that Fonso is not her father stuns Celie. It is as though someone had taken the equation of her life, multiplied by an unknown variable and left her with nothing. Celie's sense of the family unit has been negated. She must mourn for her unknown, natural father, killed unjustly, a mother who was both demented and weak, and Celie must also accept the fact that she was the victim of a sick and abusive stepfather. But, despite everything, Celie is able to state happily, "My children *not* my sister and brother." Celie was not the victim of incest.

Celie is strong enough now to confront Fonso. She has already confronted Albert's authority; now she takes on Fonso. Not only does her decision to do so reveal Celie's new strength, but it also shows that she is a Christian. Celie offers Fonso an opportunity to apologize and ask for forgiveness. Fonso, however, has no apology for Celie; time has not altered his character. In fact, at his advanced age, he has taken a fifteen-year-old wife because Celie's stepmother, May Ellen—in Fonso's words—"got too old" for him.

The imagery of flowers and spring are extensive here. The new pants outfits which Shug and Celie wear have blue floral prints. Celie writes, "Then all along the road there's Easter lilies and jonquils and daffodils and all kinds of little early wildflowers." Spring, rebirth, blooming, and the idea of beauty color Celie's life. Fonso's young wife's name is Daisy, and Shug's real name is Lilly. The world is full of wonder and possibility and beauty, but even the once-naive Celie realizes that her new world is not perfect, nor will it ever be. At the makeshift cemetery, there are weeds as well as flowers.

Letter 69 is the first letter that Celie has addressed directly to Nettie. Celie not only believes "on faith" in Nettie's existence now, but she knows that Nettie is alive, just as Celie knows that she herself is alive.

## Letters 70–72

"Unbelief is a terrible thing. And so is the hurt we cause others unknowingly," Nettie writes in an insightful and meaningful revelation. Corrine refuses to believe that Celie is the mother of Olivia and Adam; she says that she cannot even remember meeting Celie (Letter 10). In addition, Nettie realizes that Corrine is physically very ill.

"She gets weaker and weaker and unless she can believe us . . . [she will die ignorant of the truth]," Nettie emphasizes to Celie. Nettie reaches out to Celie, as Celie once reached out to God, asking for help in carrying a terrible burden. If Corrine is to die, Nettie wants her to die knowing the truth about the children's true mother. The truth, Nettie hopes, will give Corrine peace and will make Nettie no longer a socially accepted missionary "sister," but an emotionally love-linked sister, bonded by their sharing of Olivia and Adam.

Throughout the novel, as we have noted, quilts have been a source of collaboration and sisterhood. The purpose of a quilt is to take various scraps and transform them into a single, colorful, unified blanket. The tradition of making quilts is ancient. In West Africa, intricate designs and patterns were developed, and the craft was carried across the Atlantic on slave ships and transplanted in the New World. Just as creating quilts unifies Africans and Americans, and just as it unified Sofia and Celie (Letter 28), the memory of Corrine's quilts now reconciles Nettie and Corrine. Nettie searches until she finds a quilt that she hopes will remind Corrine of days long ago, when Olivia was a tiny baby and when Celie first saw her and Corrine. Nettie desperately wants "to save" Corrine from dying unhappy.

Corrine is not a bad woman, of course; she is merely dishonest and weak. In Letter 10, when she first met Celie, she lied about her reason for calling the baby Olivia. She even confesses, eventually, that she was afraid that "she'd [Celie would] want her [Olivia] back. So I forgot her as soon as I could." Being a good Christian by nature, Nettie loves and forgives Corrine for her selfish, possessive love of the children.

In Letter 49, Celie gave Shug a detailed account of Nettie; she shared this painful, precious information about Nettie with Shug because they were close, deep friends. In a similar way, Nettie now tells Samuel about Celie. Samuel and Shug are fortunate that they have been offered a chance to share in the two sisters' enormous love for one another, despite the fact that for the present, "Only the sky above us do we [Nettie and Celie] hold in common."

The bonding of women, extending even to shared sexual pleasure, has been noted earlier. Here again, in Letter 72, in a parallel to Celie and Shug's earlier intimacy, Olivia and Tashi also seem to be involved in a physical relationship. Significantly, Nettie does not think that it is morally wrong because she is sophisticated enough to realize that everyone needs intimacy, and when men are incapable of fulfilling a woman's emotional needs, there is nothing wrong in a woman turning to another woman for love and friendship.

## Letters 73–79

Having thrown off Fonso and Albert's vicious domination, Celie's newfound strength begins to crumble. *Why?* she asked God in the first letter she wrote to him, and now, she asks *why* again. Long before Job, people who were victims of injustice cried out to their gods and, when they got no answer, they did what Celie does here—that is, she seemingly renounces God. Celie has sufficient psychological distance now that she can look back on her childhood and on the numerous times that she was raped and beaten. She tries to reconcile all that physical abuse with her unflagging love and belief in God. It is little wonder that Celie wonders if God isn't, after all, "just like all the other mens I know. Trifling, forgitful and lowdown." Celie was strong when the situation called for strength; now that the crisis is past, she lets down and allows herself to feel the awful pain of injustice once again.

For the first time in the novel, Celie resents all of the unnecessary pain she has endured for decades. Significantly, Celie relates all this pain to the way that *men* have treated her. Seemingly, her faith is gone. But if faith is figuratively like flat land, and Celie's doubts and blasphemy are like debris that covers that flat land, remember that debris does *not* destroy the land. For the present, Celie thinks that God has betrayed her and ignored her; God seems to be only another callous, uncaring man.

We can accept the likelihood of Celie's feeling this way, but what catches us unaware in Letter 73 is not Celie's anger, but, in contrast, Shug's defense of God. From the beginning, Shug has been a "sinful" person—drinking, smoking, whoring, and so on. In fact, in Letter 22, the minister at church used Shug as an example of a tramp, "a strumpet in short skirts . . . singing for money and taking other women mens."

Shug's ideas about God are quite different from Celie's. Because Shug views life and the world as beautiful, she thinks that God wants all of his children to participate in life as a joyous celebration. "To please God," Shug says, "I can lay back and just admire stuff. Be happy. Have a good time." Shug thinks that it's a sin not to be happy and appreciate beauty—and, furthermore, she thinks that a person should look for beauty. Shug believes that it "pisses God off if you walk by the color purple in a field somewhere and don't notice it."

Celie's idea of God is wholly different from Shug's. Celie has suffered misery from men, and she has believed that she *had* to accept it. To her, God was just another man, up in the sky, a white man who was patiently listening to her. Now Celie believes that God allowed her to suffer and paid no attention to her prayers. She is furious. Therefore, Shug patiently has to explain, in essence, that God is not a man and certainly not a white man. God, to Shug, is everything. God is so much everything that he — or more correctly, it — cannot be visualized or expressed completely. God is not white, or black, or male. God is God. He gave Celie, Shug emphasizes, life, good health and "a good woman [Shug] that love you to death."

It is absolutely believable that Celie would believe that God was a trifling *man*. As an oppressed black American, she has been taught that white men are the superior source of authority. Likewise, God is omnipotent. For that reason, Nettie's observation that Jesus had lamb's wool-like hair (kinky) was a puzzling idea to her; that kind of hair allows for the possibility that God is black. When Celie says, "If he ever listened to poor colored women the world would be a different place," she is saying that God is white, male, and rich. Celie read Nettie's letter about Jesus' hair being kinky, but clearly, she did not believe it. Shug reinforces Celie's notion; "The last thing niggers want to think about they God is that his hair kinky," she says.

Celie's anger continues to lash out against God and against men, and, therefore, Shug, Celie's mother figure, decides that it is time to invite Celie to come to Memphis with her. Celie accepts Shug's invitation, but before she leaves, she seizes the opportunity to release once again all of the pent-up fury and frustration in her soul. Much to the astonishment of everyone, Celie tells Albert off. In her own words, she tells Albert that she's leaving, and that his dead body is "just the welcome mat" she needs to step on in order to "enter into the Creation."

In addition, Celie lashes out against Harpo, blaming him for Sofia's miserable fate. In retaliation, Harpo and Grady and Albert blame their wives for their troubles. Thus, Squeak decides to join the wives — Celie and Shug — and go to Memphis too. Squeak wants a career and independence. Shug, of course, already has an exciting career and independence.

In a parallel of Shug and Celie's relationship, in which Celie (the wife) was kind to Shug (the mistress), Sofia (the wife) is kind to Squeak (the mistress). Sofia promises to look after Squeak's child while Squeak lives in Memphis. Almost as an afterthought, Squeak advises Sofia to look after Harpo too, implying that Harpo is still part child himself.

The relationships between mistresses and wives in this novel seem rather unconventional; in most novels, wives battle mistresses, and vice versa. It is possible, however, that Walker intentionally creates relationships based on the West African tradition of polygamy, a tradition in which the wives are bonded through work and friendship as though they were sisters.

Note that Celie, Shug, and Squeak are not going to some mythical Land of Happiness in the North. At that time, there were still Jim Crow laws in the South which prohibited blacks from using the same public facilities as whites, but the women aren't "running"; they are staying in the South, driving to Memphis, through northern Georgia, "going off in the bushes," if necessary, but staying in the country they know – claiming what they can, as long as they can.

As you read Letter 76, recall Nettie's first letters describing Africa. Here, Memphis is just as exotic for Celie as Africa was for Nettie. Both sisters witness rare animals and unfamiliar living quarters; each of them has entered worlds that they never thought they would, and each of them enters by the grace of someone else's sincere kindness. Nettie was not Samuel or Corrine's maid, nor is Celie Shug's maid. Both sisters reach their full independence by striking out on their own; they celebrate their identities when they leave the plantation.

It's not every woman who can sew, but we have seen throughout the novel that Celie is an excellent seamstress. She has sewn several quilts. This is the first time, though, that she's been able to sew creatively. And for her continued growth as a woman, it is necessary for her to begin her sewing business as a pantsmaker – not a "dressmaker." Not long ago, Shug offered to sew some pants for Celie in order for her to work more easily in the fields. Now, it is Celie who is sewing pants for Shug to wear when she sings on stage. Celie proves to be just as good a seamstress as Shug is a songstress. Both women are "originals"; before Celie sewed up her idea, nobody ever made "folkspants" before.

Returning to the plantation, in Letter 78, Celie has "visitor status" now, as opposed to member status. Albert does not even recognize her when he sees her. She looks pretty, feels great, and has smoked

58

marijuana in order to get closer to God. She has Shug to thank for introducing her to both getting high and theism. "Girl, I'm bless. God know what I mean."

Harpo, we see, has become more of a father to Albert than he ever was a son to him. After Celie left, he even bathed Albert, comforting him and holding him in his arms. Albert suffered a kind of emotional stroke when he realized that Shug and Celie left him for each other. Recall that in Letter 74, Celie cursed him, vowing that he would suffer, just as he made her suffer. Albert has suffered; we can believe that he has experienced frustration, humiliation, and depression, and he seems ready to change. Harpo has even made Albert give Celie the rest of Nettie's letters.

## Letters 80 & 81

Letter 80 is a rich storehouse of all the themes of the novel. The three most significant themes discussed are male and female relationships, African and black American relationships, and personal independence.

Concerning the second of these themes, you should be aware that Samuel and Nettie (now that Corrine is dead) are good missionaries, but they have no sense of place; they don't belong. They belong neither to the world of the European power structure nor to the traditional world of the black West African. They belong only to God and to one another. In the world of growing avarice and exploitation that is encroaching into the jungle, they are powerless. Samuel is disappointed that the Olinka never recognized them as blood brother and sister. In fact, the Olinka reject Samuel and Nettie, suspicious of their rejection of America's "progress" – motorcars, for example.

Had Samuel and Nettie not have gotten married, they both may have ended up feeling completely unappreciated. Samuel's character has the distinction of being the only accepting, loving and giving husband in the entire novel.

The mention of "DuBoyce" in this letter is important. Nettie is actually discussing the great black American sociologist, philosopher, and civil rights leader, W. E. B. DuBois, who was born in 1868 and died in 1963 in Ghana, West Africa. As a noted scholar, he tried to create an appreciation of black Americans, and he was instrumental in founding the National Association for the Advancement of Colored People (NAACP). He and Booker T. Washington, the founder of

Tuskegee Institute in Tuskegee, Alabama, had a heated debate over the method by which blacks should advance. Washington stressed a practical economic freedom which would in time lead to a political and cultural freedom. Washington wanted blacks to get jobs as postal workers, carpenters, and repairmen. On the other hand, DuBois wanted blacks to aspire to become professionals. His Harvard education made him fiercely defend the position that knowledge was the most important thing a man could acquire.

Walker presents DuBois accurately in *The Color Purple* because he certainly would have been appalled at Aunt Theodosia's ignorance. He was a very austere, serious, and self-righteous man.

Doris Baines is a clever woman who has made herself happy in Africa. Writing saved her life. It is interesting that she chooses to call Harold her "grandson" for he is no blood relation to her. Since he is the offspring of one of her "wives," then he should be her "son." But Doris Baines thinks of her two "wives" as her daughters. She is delighted with the fact that she was a mystery to both the natives and her readers. She uses a male pseudonym and has two "wives," it is true, but she is no freak; she is a lively and kind woman.

Turning to Adam's infatuation with Tashi, we should recall Harpo's initial infatuation with Sofia. Here, Nettie is acting very much in the same capacity that Celie once did with Harpo long ago. Like Harpo, Adam believes himself to be deeply in love with Tashi, who is just as independent as Sofia was.

And similarly, just as Sofia was beaten in prison, Tashi is beaten during her female rite of passage; afterward, Nettie describes Tashi as looking "listless, dull-eyed and tired." When we compare Nettie's description of Tashi with Celie's description of Sofia in Letter 37, it is difficult to tell which woman was more mutilated.

Nettie closes Letter 81 with a sentence that magnifies the radiance of her sisterhood with Celie; she says, "But all things look brighter because I have a loving soul to share them with."

### Letters 82–85

With Fonso's death, Nettie and Celie can enjoy financial security, a matter that the two sisters never considered before; in fact, they have never before had any place that they could call "home." In keeping with her basic, sturdy humility, Celie has never even thought about having a home of her own (homes always "belonged" to men), but the quick cedar smoke exorcism that she and Shug perform is a simple and powerful way of showing that Evil (of which Fonso is the most dramatic personification) has been purged from her life.

Evil has been purged, perhaps, but not pain. Very quickly, Celie is pained by Shug's taking a new lover, a male. Once again a man brings pain to Celie. For Walker to have made Shug doggedly loyal to Celie, however, would have been unrealistic. Shug enjoys men. She enjoys and loves Celie, but she enjoys men too, and she knows that eventually Germaine will hurt her "worse than I'm hurting you [Celie]." Shug needs a "last fling." Celie cannot understand Shug's needs, though. Celie is a simple woman, one who has been hurt very often and very deeply.

Albert, too, has been hurt, and he has suffered. While we watch him and Celie tending to Henrietta, we realize that not only does caring for the girl keep Celie going, but that it gives meaning to Albert's life. Suffering and a developing concern for Henrietta are slowly re-forming Albert. But without Shug, neither Celie's nor Albert's lives is complete. Albert even tries to confront Celie with the truth about her aversion to him, but Celie cannot bring herself to utter the truth. Albert asks Celie if she rejects him because he is a man; Celie never tells him precisely that, yes, she rejects him because he is a man, but that is her reason. In fact, men are less than human to Celie. They are "frogs." No man has ever given Celie pure love. Only women have done that for Celie.

At the moment when Celie seems to be at her lowest emotional bottom, she receives a telegram from the Department of Defense, stating that Nettie and the children are dead. Then all of Celie's letters to Nettie are returned unopened, taking Celie even further into the depths of depression. This depression, though, will be the measure of Celie's final joy when, at last, she experiences the peak of ecstasy: her reunion with her beloved sister, Nettie.

## Letter 86

However far apart Nettie and Celie have been, they have managed to remain spiritual twins. Nearly thirty years have passed. Nettie doesn't know if Celie is even alive, but the memory and the emotions associated with Celie are alive – and that's what matters. In a similar way, the "image" of God is no longer important to Nettie. She doesn't think of God as a gentle old white man, as many black Americans do; instead, God is different, she tells Celie. He is "more spirit than ever before . . . not being tied to what God looks like, frees us."

An unfortunate aspect of Nettie's not having received Celie's letters is that she does not know that Fonso has died and that they are heirs to the land. Nettie thinks that she and Celie will be poor for many more years, and that it "will be years no doubt before we even own a home." But Nettie never loses hope and the dream of reunion with Celie. The words of their letters bind them together, and the words of their prayers for one another's well-being make their love for one another even stronger.

## Letter 87

Celie has finally matured sufficiently to separate her miserable existence and her rich inner world into two separate spheres: the physical world and the emotional world. Celie's body may be aging and going through menopause, but her feelings, in contrast, are ever spring-like: "My heart [is] young and fresh; it feel like it blooming blood." Remember that Celie did not understand menstruation in Letter 8, but she clearly understands the process of menopause here. Another example of Celie's emotional growth can be measured by her dismissal of the news of Nettie's alleged death in Letter 85. "And I don't believe you dead. How can you be dead if I still feel you?"

In addition, Celie no longer hates Albert. In Letter 74, she called him a "lowdown dog," denounced him, and decided to leave with Shug. Now, however, both Albert and Celie have been replaced in Shug's life by youthful Germaine. "Here us is, I thought, two old fools left over from love." They are in an unplanned union. The husband had a mistress who stole his wife from him, and now that mistress has left both of them for a younger man. Albert partially understands Celie's feelings of rejection, and she, in turn, acknowledges his misery. "I don't hate him for two reasons. One, he love Shug. And two, Shug use to love him." Shug is the magical ingredient that makes the difference for Celie.

Sofia, meanwhile, has learned to compromise. She tells Eleanor Jane that it's "too late to cry." Instead, she says, "All us can do is laugh." Celie's words are much like Sofia's words. Sofia feels helpless, but she can still laugh – despite everything. Celie, likewise, has accepted her position socially and emotionally. She is an aging black woman and says, "I try to teach my heart not to want nothing it can't have."

This letter is one of the longest and most complex letters in the novel. Not only is there the well-developed contrast between the physical and the emotional worlds of the characters, but there is also a letter within a letter, and note that Shug's letter to Celie is not unlike one of Nettie's letters to Celie. Shug's son James faces many of the same problems on the Indian reservation that Samuel and Nettie faced among the Olinka. He is an outsider who is oppressed by the ruling power structure.

Shug is now a grandmother, although her parents have reared her three children. Celie doesn't mind; she loves Shug even if Shug isn't young anymore. She loves Shug best, she admits, because of "what she [Shug] has been through." We, in turn, love Celie because she has survived what she has been through; Celie is a survivor, and no one in the novel has undergone more injustice and unhappiness than Celie.

Even Albert is able to honestly acknowledge the reason why he beat Celie; as we have noted before, he beat her because she was not Shug—a wholly irrational excuse. Albert also admits that he loved Shug because of her independence; for that reason, he also admits that he never understood the relationship between Shug and Celie. With this in mind, recall Letter 64. There, Nettie told Celie how the many wives of an Olinka man became friends, and she explained how those friendships excluded the husband. Interestingly, neither the Olinka husbands nor Albert is able to understand the special bonds between women, especially between women who share the same man.

## Letter 88

Nettie's assumption in Letter 86 that her nephew, Adam, went looking for Tashi in the forest was correct. Adam and Tashi intend to marry. Here, it is profitable to remember back to Harpo's first feelings of love. Adam seems to feel very much as Harpo did long ago, except that Adam is more intelligent and more gentle. Similarly, Tashi's boldness and reluctance to marry Adam are very much like young Sofia's attitude and actions. The difference, however, is that Adam is willing to change for Tashi. Harpo refused to change, even though we know that he loved her. Adam's visit to the *mbeles* and his scarring his face not only show his deep love for Tashi, but his love and respect for African blackness, as well.

## Letters 89 & 90

Each of the last twenty letters of this novel has contained reversals. Shug has run off with Germaine. Celie and Albert have been reunited. Harpo now does all the housework, and Sofia works outside the home. In this letter, yet another reversal takes place, a sociological reversal. Eleanor Jane, a white woman and the daughter of the mayor, works for Sofia ("Whoever heard of a white woman working for niggers?"). In Letter 37, remember, Sofia was imprisoned for not wanting to be a maid to a white woman. Now, one of the children whom Sofia helped rear is helping to look after Henrietta and do cooking. Sofia too has become less bold and brassy; she has changed. Once, Sofia had a "the-hell-with-heaven" attitude; now, after having been through "hell," in and out of prison, and having been beaten like a dog, she can believe in a better life. "Everybody learn something in life," she admits.

Albert's transformation also becomes complete. Not only does he become "one of the women" by sewing with Celie, but he is now able to express his feelings honestly and without meanness. "The more I wonder, the more I love," he tells Celie.

Albert and Celie have places reserved for Shug not only in their hearts, but in their homes. Shug is family to Celie and Albert, and likewise Shug "adopts" people; after Shug has affairs and has ended them, her ex-lovers become "family" to her. Shug and Germaine try to investigate the alleged death of Nettie, and later, Shug sends Germaine to attend Wilberforce University, a small, predominantly black school in Wilberforce, Ohio, because she "can't let all that talent go to waste." Shug has no lover or husband now, but she has friends who are family to her.

Finally, in Letter 90, two sisters who were not allowed to grow up together are reunited, and for the rest of their lives, they will live together, and they will die together. There is nothing in this final letter that suggests that Celie is only imagining their reunion. Therefore, the report of Nettie's death in Letter 85 was wrong.

Recall that in Letter 87, Celie said, "My heart must be young and fresh . . . it feel like it blooming blood." This same feeling is infused in her words here: "But I don't think us feel old at all. And us so happy. Matter of fact, I think this the youngest us ever felt."

Celie's love for Nettie provides her with an inexhaustible source of youth. When she and Nettie embrace, Nettie never asks Celie why she did not write. Celie doesn't tell Nettie about Albert's interception of her letters, and Nettie doesn't ask Celie if she learned "to fight." There is no need to. Their letters and feelings, along with their prayers, have already provided this information. All they have to do now is introduce their "peoples" to each other.

# CHARACTER ANALYSES

## CELIE

When the novel opens, Celie is a young black girl living in Georgia in the early years of the twentieth century. She is largely uneducated; her letters to God are written in non-standard dialect. Walker has called the dialect black folk language, and while it may not be polished English, it is raw and honest — and strong. Celie's letters are unusually strong; they are evidence of an unusual strength in a very young woman. They are evidence of Celie's painful struggle to hold on — despite all of the multiple horrors of her life.

Celie is about to go into adolescence, believing that she was raped by her father and that he killed both of their children. She writes to God because she has no one else to help her bear this terrible knowledge. What has happened to Celie is so terrible that she can talk about it only to someone whom she feels loves her. Of course, her sister, Nettie, loves her, but Nettie is too young to understand what terrible things have happened to Celie. Only to God can Celie talk honestly and openly about the hell that she has suffered.

And this point is important: Celie is not complaining to God. She simply needs to talk to someone — someone whom she loves and trusts and someone whom she feels loves her.

Celie's instinct for survival, however, is more solid than even Celie realizes. She was born into a poor family; her mother was ill much of the time (later, we find out that she was mentally ill as well); there were too many children in the family; and then Celie was victimized by the man whom she believed was her father. Celie feels used, and she feels that she is a victim, and she doesn't understand why all this has happened to her. She doesn't complain; she simply wonders why. In fact, so many bad things have happened to Celie that she feels worthless. She has very little self-worth and self-esteem. You should notice that she doesn't even sign her letters to God. Normally, most people take pride in signing their names; our name is one of the first things we learn to write. This is not true of Celie. Her self-worth is so miniscule that she does not even sign her own name.

Slowly, Celie will mature into a woman of enormous confidence — but not before her beloved sister Nettie is taken from her and not before she herself is married to a cruel man who really wanted to marry Nettie.

For a time, Celie is more a slave to her husband than she is a wife. And then a near-miracle happens. Her husband's mistress, Shug, comes to the house to recuperate and Celie becomes her nurse. By nature, Shug is a strong woman; men don't tangle with Shug, unless she wants them to—in bed. As Shug grows stronger physically, and as Celie nurses her, Shug encourages Celie to grow stronger psychologically. Similarly, Celie's daughter-in-law Sofia shows Celie how to stand up to men and how to stand up to prejudice and injustice—and fight.

It isn't easy for Celie to learn how to verbalize her independence, and it is harder still for her to act on these new concepts, but after she discovers how intentionally cruel her husband has been to her, she rebels and throws off her role as a slave to her husband.

By the end of the novel, Celie's newfound strength, as well as her ever-enduring love for Nettie, pays off. All through the years, she has kept the memory of Nettie alive, despite the fact that there was no proof that Nettie was alive. Nettie not only is alive, but she helped raise Celie's two children, and when the book ends, Celie and Nettie and Celie's two children, now grown, are reunited. Despite all the odds, Celie held on. She learned to fight, to stand up for herself, and she was rewarded. She never gave up on her love for Nettie, nor did she give up on her love for God. Celie survived physically and spiritually, and she matured into a full, solid, modern twentieth-century woman.

Many critics of the novel have been annoyed and repelled by the content of the book's opening letter to God. The idea of beginning a novel with the fact of a rape is repugnant to them. Walker's answer is straight to the point. "This is the country in which a woman is raped every three minutes," she says, "where one out of three women will be raped during their lifetimes and a quarter of those are children under 12."

There is no delicate, glossy way to introduce the subject of rape. Accordingly, Walker handles it head-on, immediately. After we have accepted the horror of what we read, we can stand back in awe at Celie's continuing courage in the face of what she has to endure, and we can particularly admire her continuing, sustaining love for her sister, Nettie. This book isn't about rape. It is about what happens after rape.

In fact, one of the central focuses of the book is on Celie's mental and emotional rebirth. Hate and violence have almost killed Celie, but then she meets Shug, a woman who is able to kindle feelings of sexual love and self-love within Celie – for the first time. In a similar way, Celie becomes friends with her daughter-in-law, who teaches her by example what courage is.

The strength of these women, and their caring for one another, offer opportunities for all three of them to continue growing – despite the racist, sexist world they live in. During the course of the book, they cry together, laugh together, affirm life together, and share one another's joys. They respect one another. They live together in a world that Celie could never have imagined when she was fourteen; in fact, it is a world that she never could have imagined until, ironically, her husband brought home his ailing mistress. Never did Albert imagine the mental and physical sense of new health that Shug, his mistress, would bring to Celie. Because of Shug and because of Sofia, Celie is able to triumph – and triumph joyfully – over the sexual and racial oppression that smothered many of her female ancestors.

*The Color Purple*, then, is a story about growth, endurance, loyalty, solidarity, and joy – all nurtured by the strength of love.

## SHUG AVERY

Initially, Shug Avery seems little more than a flashy blues singer who is not only selfish, but also arrogant. However, the key to Shug's character is the element of surprise: Shug always catches us off-guard. In particular, we never expect the self-centered and seemingly superficial Shug to awaken love and self-esteem in Celie, and we certainly never expect Celie to awaken generosity in Shug.

However, just as Celie has never had the opportunity to recognize the potential of herself, Shug has tried to avoid realizing the truth about who she herself is. For example, Shug discarded her name – "Lilly" – and adopted the nickname (not a real name) of "Shug," suggesting a bite of super-sweetness, a quality which is exactly diametrical to the "real" Shug. Shug, in fact, refuses to be "sweet"; she is uncompromisingly honest. Her first words to Celie are, "You sure *is* ugly."

Later, however, Shug befriends Celie, and still later, she becomes her lover. A psychologist would probably classify Shug as bisexual, but the terminology isn't important. The significance of Celie and Shug's sexual relationship is that Celie learns how to be proud of her body and that she learns how to use it to enjoy sex.

Celie, in fact, is probably Shug's only authentic friend. Shug, by nature, is manipulative and superficially popular – a free spirit. When Shug is ill, none of the people who seem to enjoy her singing come to see her; they enjoy her music more than they like her. Even her lover, Albert, Celie's husband, doesn't take care of her; he gives her to Celie to care for. Shug, like Celie, never had much affection in her life, especially when she was growing up in Memphis, and although Shug and Albert have three children, Shug is not a "mother." Shug only becomes a "mother" when she begins to love and respond to the warmth that she sees in Celie.

One of the qualities that makes Shug such a "natural" in this novel is the fact that Walker did not, by accident, decide to make Shug a blues singer. Clearly, Shug's being a blues singer is central to her character. The blues are the simplest form of jazz – like "Shug" is the simplest form of "sugar." And the word "jazz" itself comes from a West African word meaning, literally, sperm – and, figuratively, life. In turn, Shug brings a sense of life to her audiences with her singing, and, of course, she brings Celie to life.

Shug is full of life on stage, and she seems to live a sweet life, for the most part, because she enjoys shaking and crooning. However, Shug's "blues" dimension is defined by her selfishness – which leads to lonely isolation. In fact, her love for Albert is reduced to a simple, physical longing for him. He has slighted her twice – by not marrying her initially, and again by not marrying her after Annie Julia died. Shug resents Albert's slighting her; she may be a black woman, but she doesn't want to be defined by someone else's sense of a black woman's worth, or in Albert's particular case, by his sense of a black woman's non-worth.

By nature, especially in her singing, Shug is a "changer"; she starts singing the blues, then turns to a fast snappy ragtime tune. Jazz by its very nature is lovely, unpredictable, and improvisational, and Shug is jazzy because she invents rules and cannot be contained. She is

originality. She is a changer, and she effects the most change, ultimately, not on herself, but on Celie.

By being an original, a unique kind of black woman in this novel,
one of the things that strikes us most forcefully about Shug is her
original concept of God—particularly when compared to the limited
concept of the God whom Celie believes in. Shug realizes that although
churchgoers may condemn her and her glowing lifestyle, God himself,
or itself, does *not* condemn her—because he, or it, is everything. Shug
postulates that it is a sin to be miserable and unappreciative of the
world and its beauty.

Finally, Shug is the color purple personified. She is both red and
blue simultaneously. Red represents jazz and life, and the blues' origins
are in misery and disappointment. Together, red and blue create
purple.

## ALBERT/MR. _____

Albert is not easy to understand. His character is at once evil and
weak. One usually thinks of an evil person as being a strong person,
but in Albert's case, this is not true. He is weak and he is evil. His
mistreatment of Celie is unthinkable today—and totally unnecessary.
And yet his adoration of Shug Avery humanizes him.

Of all the central ideas in this novel, the key to understanding
many of the characters lies in their lack of self-knowledge and in their
gradually learning to know themselves and value themselves. This
is certainly true in Albert's case. The roots of his evil nature come
from his not knowing himself. Albert's father didn't rear him to be
independent, but rather to be subservient to his father's own interests.
When Albert became a man, he used his father for a role model and
evolved into a self-centered, irrational individual.

For example, note that Albert never asks Shug to marry him,
although he declares his love for her openly. In contrast, his first wife
was driven to take a lover because she received so little attention from
Albert. It is possible that Albert is both very frightened and very awed
by Shug. If this is true, then perhaps he was too afraid to ask her to
marry him. He couldn't control her. She ruled the relationship. She
came to him when she wanted to be involved with him. Eventually
Albert does go to Shug, but he waits—until Shug is weak and sick.
Then he goes to her and brings her to his home. But note that he is
totally unconcerned about what his dutiful wife, Celie, will think. It

is *his* house. Albert is much more concerned with what Shug will think and that her health will improve.

Albert, of course, never really wanted to marry Celie. When he first approached Fonso, Celie and Nettie's stepfather, it was Nettie whom he wanted to marry. Nettie was not flashy like Shug, but she was pretty and young. Fonso opted to marry off Celie instead. Celie wasn't "valuable"; she wasn't a virgin. Nettie was. Albert had to take second-best, Fonso's "spoiled" daughter.

In assessing Albert's character, one always returns, ultimately, to his cruelty to Celie. Celie suffers terribly at Albert's hands. He beats her because she is not Shug. He hides the letters that Nettie writes to Celie to hurt both Nettie and Celie. He is not strong enough to tell Celie that Nettie refused his offer and fought off his sexual advances. Instead, he hides Nettie's letters, an act which defines him indelibly as a coward.

Albert has sex with Celie in a callous and uncaring way. He cares little about her pleasure. However, when Albert is with Shug, he is obviously an expert and exciting lover.

In the course of the novel, Albert is completely reformed. He goes from being the mean, anonymous Mr. _____, a detestable figure, to being an understanding, grandfatherly figure. The key to this transformation lies in the misery he experiences when both Shug and Celie leave him. The reason for his character reversal is that Celie finally becomes a person in her own right. She becomes independent and full of love. The transformation in Celie allows Albert to realize that his meanness cheated him from enjoying the wonderful new Celie during the years that they were married.

## SOFIA

Sofia is strong, fierce, and daring to a fault. In fact, it is her refusal to lessen or belittle herself that almost leads to her destruction.

As a black American woman reared in the South in the 1930s, she rejects completely the systematic oppression that engulfed the position of the black woman. In that system, a black person had to remain absolutely subservient to whites—economically and socially. Blacks worked for whites, who paid them very little. In addition, a black woman came under the rule of her husband. A black woman was a virtual prisoner in the system. White men controlled the state, and black men controlled the black households. Sofia had no chance in such a setting. She simply wasn't suited for it by her very nature.

Sofia is younger than Celie, which partially explains why she is unable to accept the confining role laid out by the system for the "meek" black maid and the "dutiful" black wife. Sofia was meant to rule – not to take orders.

She fights back when Harpo tries to rule her with an iron fist. She wants a partnership relationship in their marriage, not a master-servant relationship. Sofia is a devoted mother and an excellent sister to her sisters, and she is generously forgiving. She even befriends Squeak, her husband's mistress, by volunteering to rear her child until Squeak is able to establish herself as a blues singer.

After Celie advises her stepson Harpo to beat Sofia into submission, Sofia confronts her. They are eventually reconciled, of course, but Sofia is thoroughly honest with others, as well as with herself. In contrast, when Celie admits – only to herself – that she wronged Sofia by telling Harpo to beat her, Sofia demands that Celie admit aloud that she told Harpo to beat her.

Although Sofia survives severe beatings during her imprisonment, she pays much too much for being herself, and in the process, she loses much of her strength and dignity. It is ironic that the value which she places on fighting back is the very thing that prevents her from living an independent life. Her adamant refusal to be a white woman's maid is eventually crushed, and she is forced to work – first, without pay in the prison, doing laundry, and then, with pay, as the white mayor's family maid. It is no wonder that she becomes a stranger to her own children. But it is to Harpo's credit that he loves Sofia more than anything, and he has a lasting love for her which proves that he respects her personhood.

In summary, Sofia is not tragic as much as she is symbolic of a woman who had the courage to fight against known odds.

## SUGGESTED IDEAS FOR ESSAYS

1. How does the death of Celie's mother change Celie's relationship with her family, with herself, and with God?

2. In what ways are Nettie and Celie different? In what ways are they similar? Does Shug replace Nettie in Celie's life?

3. What justification, if any, do Fonso and Mr. _____ have for treating Celie the way that they do?

4. In Letter 10, Celie says, "I seen my baby girl. I knowed it was her." Why is she so sure? How does she go about finding her baby?

5. In Letter 14, when it is announced that Shug is coming to town, why are both Mr. _____ and Celie so happy?

6. Keeping in mind that Celie's husband, Mr. _____, has a classic villainous character, how can you explain his hiding Nettie's letters to Celie instead of destroying them?

7. How do Nettie's letters differ from Celie's? How are they the same?

8. Sofia is unjustly imprisoned. How is this related to the major theme of injustice which touches all of the main characters in the novel?

9. In Letter 68, Shug is insistent that Celie come to Memphis with her. Why is Celie so confused and shocked? Why does she feel released from her life with Mr. _____?

10. How are Celie's letters like prayers? Explain her reasons for writing, "Dear Nettie, I don't write to God no more, I write to you. What happen to God? ast Shug. Who that? I say." (Letter 73). How does this quotation contrast with the first lines of the novel, "You better not never tell nobody but God."? In Letter 90, why does Celie address all of her world and God twice?

11. Explain the relationship between the color of purple and the feeling of beauty.

12. Examine the effect of two "arranged" marriages—Celie's to Albert, and Albert's to Annie Julia—and the consequences of each of them.

# SELECTED BIBLIOGRAPHY

## Book Reviews

MORT, M. E. *Library Journal* 107:1115 (June 1, 1982).

PRESCOTT, P. S. *Newsweek* 99:67 (June 21, 1982).

WATKINS, MEL. *New York Times Book Review* (June 25, 1982).

## Film Reviews

BLAKE, R. A. *America* 154:75 (February 1, 1986).

KAUFFMANN, S. *New Republic* 194:24–5 (January 27, 1986).

NORMENT, L. *Ebony* 41:146+ (February, 1986).

O'BRIEN, T. *Commonweal* 113:52–3 (January 31, 1986).

SIMON, J. *National Review* 38:56–7 (February 14, 1986).

TRAVERS, P. *People Weekly* 25:18 (January 6, 1986).

## Books and Articles

_____. "Alice Walker Goes Home." *Jet* 69:27–30 (February 10, 1986).

_____. "Blacks in Movies." *Jet* (February 10, 1986).

ANELLO, R. "Characters in Search of a Book." *Newsweek* 99:67 (June 21, 1982).

BOGLE, DONALD. *Toms, Coons, Mulattoes, Mammies, and Bucks: An Interpretive History of Blacks in American Films.* New York: Viking, 1973.

BRADLEY, D. "Telling the Black Woman's Story." *New York Times Magazine* 24–37 (January 8, 1984).

COOKE, MICHAEL G. *The Achievement of Intimacy.* New Haven: Yale University Press, 1984.

COUGHLAN, MARGARET N. *Folklore from Africa to the United States.* Washington: Library of Congress, 1976.

DAVIS, DANIEL S. *Marcus Garvey.* New York: Watts, 1972.

DILLARD, JOEY LEE. *A Lexicon of Black English.* New York: Seabury Press, 1977.

DUBOIS, WILLIAM E. B. *The Souls of Black Folk.* New York: Dodd, Mead, 1979.

DWORKIN, S. "The Strange and Wonderful Story of the Making of 'The Color Purple'." *Ms.* 14:66–70+ (December, 1985).

GIBSON, DONALD B. and CAROL ANSELMENT, eds. *Black and White: Stories of American Life.* New York: Washington Square Press, 1971.

GOLDSTEIN, W. "Alice Walker on the Set of 'The Color Purple'." *Publishers Weekly* 228:46–8 (September 6, 1985).

GUTMAN, HERBERT G. *The Black Family in Slavery and Freedom.* New York: Pantheon, 1976.

HARLAN, LOUIS R. *Booker T. Washington.* New York: Oxford University Press, 1983.

HUGHES, LANGSTON. *A Pictorial History of Blackamericans.* New York: Crown Publishers, 1983.

KING, ANITA. *Quotations in Black.* Westport, Conn.: Greenwood Press, 1981.

LOW, W. AUGUSTUS. *Encyclopedia of Black America.* New York: McGraw-Hill, 1981.

74

MOORE, CARMEN, *Somebody's Angel Child: The Story of Bessie Smith.* New York: Crowell, 1969.

OLIVER, PAUL. *Songstresses and Saints.* New York: Cambridge University Press, 1984.

PETERS, MARGARET. *The Ebony Book of Black Achievement.* Chicago: Johnson Publishers, 1974.

SHEPARD, RAY A. *Conjure Tales.* New York: Heritage, Dutton, 1973.

SMYTHE, MABEL M. *The Black American Reference Book.* Englewood Cliffs, New Jersey: Prentice-Hall, 1976.

STERLING, D. *We Are Your Sisters.* New York: Norton, 1984.

THUM, MARCELLA. *Exploring Black America.* New York: Atheneum, 1975.

WALKER, ALICE. "America Should Have Closed Down on the First Day a Black Woman Observed that Supermarket Collard Greens Tasted like Water." *Ms.* 13:53+ (January, 1985).

_____. "Embracing the Dark and the Light." *Essence* 13:67+ (January, 1982).

_____. "Finding Celie's Voice." *Ms.* 14:71–2+ (December, 1985).

WALLACE, MICHELE. *Black Macho and the Myth of the Superwoman.* New York: Dial Press, 1979.

WASHINGTON, M. H. "Alice Walker: Her Mother's Gifts." *Ms.* (June, 1982).

# NOTES

**NOTES**